Southeastern Wetlands

A GUIDE TO SELECTED SITES IN GEORGIA, NORTH CAROLINA, SOUTH CAROLINA, TENNESSEE, AND KENTUCKY

TEXT BY **Parke Puterbaugh**

PHOTOGRAPHY BY **John Netherton**

AND **Tom Blagden, Jr.**

CO-PUBLISHED BY THE
U.S. ENVIRONMENTAL PROTECTION AGENCY
AND THE TENNESSEE VALLEY AUTHORITY

Co-published by: U.S. Environmental Protection Agency
and Tennessee Valley Authority

Editor: Jennifer Derby, EPA
Copy Editor: Jo Ann Fowler, TVA
Packager: Suzanne Venino
Designer: Rebecca Finkel, F + P Graphic Design

ISBN: 0-9659726-0-7
EPA Number: 904-B-97-901
Text: © Parke Puterbaugh, 1997. All rights reserved.
Photography: © John Netherton, 1997. All rights reserved.
© Tom Blagden, Jr., 1997. All rights reserved
Maps: © Rebecca Finkel, 1997. All rights reserved.
Art: © A. B. Forster, 1997. All rights reserved.

Printed in Hong Kong

Publisher's Cataloging-in-Publication

Puterbaugh, Parke.
  Southeastern wetlands : a guide to selected sites in Georgia,
North Carolina, South Carolina, Tennessee and Kentucky / written
by Parke Puterbaugh ; photography by John Netherton and Tom
Blagden, Jr. — 1st ed.
  p. cm.
  ISBN: 0-9659726-0-7
  1. Wetlands—Southern States—Recreational use—
Guidebooks. 2. Wetlands ecology—Southern States—
Guidebooks. I. Netherton, John. II. Blagden, Tom. III. Title

GV191.42.A135P88 1997   333.78'09768
                                          QBI97-41054

Cover: Tidal marsh along the Edisto River, ACE Basin, South Carolina, by Tom Blagden, Jr.
First frontispiece: Cypress trees, Reelfoot Lake, Tennessee, by John Netherton
Second frontispiece: Marsh along the Edisto River, ACE Basin, South Carolina, by Tom Blagden, Jr.

Glossy ibis on Bear Island,
ACE Basin, South Carolina
Tom Blagden, Jr.

Acknowledgments

Exploring Southeastern wetlands was a dream assignment, but it is not something I could have done without assistance. I would like to thank the following people for generously sharing their time, knowledge, and enthusiasm during the researching of this book:

Mike Allison, Marc Evans, Deborah White (Blanton Forest); Tom Biebigauser (Cave Run Lake); Jim Burkhart, Maggie O'Connell (Okefenokee Swamp); Mike Dawson, Lawrence Sisk (Francis Beidler Forest); Linda Gintolli, Brad Smith (Green Swamp Preserve); Rick Ingram, Michael Housh (Carolina Sandhills); Kathy Ludlow, Megan Martoglio (Badin Upland Depression Swamps); Jerry McCollum, F. G. Courtney (Alcovy River); Kathy McKay, Rick Clark, Fran Rametta (Congaree Swamp); Chris Meggs, Carlton Smith (Turnbull State Forest); Mike Prevost (ACE Basin); Dick Rightmeyer, Dave Jensen, Carlton Jones (Chattooga River); Larry Smith (Wolf River); John Stanton, John Ann Shearer (Lake Mattamuskeet); Keith Tassin, Christi Lambert (Altamaha River); Raymond Thomas, Barry Ellis (Skidaway Island); Floyd Williams (Merchants Millpond); Mark Williams, Troy Littrell (Reelfoot Lake).

I would also like to thank Jennifer Derby, EPA Region 4, for her tireless support and enthusiasm—not to mention thinking up the idea in the first place! Thanks also to Tim Meeks, TVA, for providing administrative and editorial support for the project. A special note of gratitude is due my wife, Carol, for tolerating frequent absences while I was out slogging around in the wild. Finally, a word of appreciation to Professor Ed Kuenzler, formerly of the University of North Carolina at Chapel Hill, who imparted both a knowledge of and enthusiasm for wetlands that has remained with me.

— PARKE PUTERBAUGH

I would like to thank the following EPA wetlanders for their valuable technical review and assistance with this publication: Bill Ainslie, Thomas Burnett, Jim Couch, Marjan Farzaad, Veronica Fasselt, Becky Fox, Gail Harrison, Eric Hughes, Morgan Jackson, Haynes Johnson, Pete Kalla, Reese Kilgore, Eva Long, Bob Lord, José Negron, Lee Pelej, Tracy Shellhorse, and Mike Wylie. Many thanks to Tom Welborn for his technical review and his unwavering support for this project.

Thanks also to Keenan and Kiersten Derby for frequent consultations on photography selection and cover design. Special thanks to Jo Ann Fowler, TVA, for her wonderful energy, thoroughness, and dedication as copy editor. Many thanks to Rebecca Finkel for her creative and artistic work designing the layout of the book. Finally, I would like to thank the packager, Suzanne Venino, for her creativity, commitment, and professionalism.

— JENNIFER DERBY

Contents

Southeastern Wetlands

Cave Run Lake
Frankfort

KENTUCKY

Blanton Forest

Reelfoot Lake

Nashville

TENNESSEE

Wolf River

Chattooga River

Atlanta

Alcovy River Greenway

GEORGIA

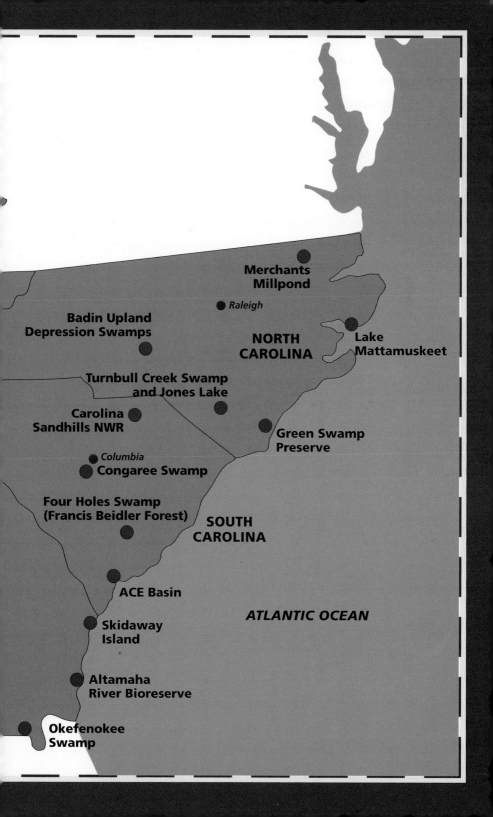

Merchants
Millpond

● Raleigh

Badin Upland
Depression Swamps

NORTH
CAROLINA

Lake
Mattamuskeet

Turnbull Creek Swamp
and Jones Lake

Carolina
Sandhills NWR

Green Swamp
Preserve

Columbia
Congaree Swamp

Four Holes Swamp
(Francis Beidler Forest)

SOUTH
CAROLINA

ACE Basin

ATLANTIC OCEAN

Skidaway
Island

Altamaha
River Bioreserve

Okefenokee
Swamp

Foreword

The Southeast still has a remarkable beauty and diversity of wetlands, as is so well illustrated by the author and photographers of this book. The challenges faced in preserving our wetlands and in protecting their health are immense—and sometimes seemingly insurmountable—because of our ever-expanding population and resource-hungry lifestyles. There are, however, community members and landowners here in the Southeast and in other parts of the country who are working to develop an awareness and appreciation for what we have lost as well as for what remains, and who are taking creative actions to protect and restore wetland environments near their homes and communities. Some of their stories are described in this book.

Fortunately, also, the children of our generation are being taught more about the environment and stewardship than have recent generations—offering promise for new perspectives and solutions to living in our natural environment in a balanced and respectful way. Still, the best lessons for children and adults alike can be learned by experiencing firsthand these wet places and other natural environments. We hope that this book will help those who are seeking such experiences.

—JENNIFER DERBY
U.S. Environmental Protection Agency

Freshwater marsh along the banks of Lake Mattamuskeet, North Carolina
John Netherton

Preface

The basic purpose of this book is to invite and inspire readers to visit wetlands. By encouraging people to get their feet wet, it is hoped that a broader cross section of the public will come to appreciate the beauty, usefulness, and desirability of wetlands. Another goal is to educate readers about the wide range of environments that are classified as wetlands. By the end of this book, you will have read about oceans, lakes, rivers, bogs, swamps, seeps, savannas, and much more.

You will also learn a fundamental truth about the somewhat misleading term "wetlands," which is that an area does not have to be constantly under water to be classified as a wetland. Though the definition is subject to ongoing debate and interpretation, what makes a wetland is determined by hydrology (the inflow and outflow of water and the height of the water table), soil (wetland soils are hydric, which is to say they lack oxygen near the surface, allowing organic matter to accumulate), and vegetation (wetland plants exhibit characteristics of both aquatic and terrestrial communities, being adapted to varying degrees of inundation).

Plant makeup may be the best way to identify a wetland. The U.S. Army Corps of Engineers made it the cornerstone of their 1987 definition of wetlands: "Those areas that are inundated or saturated by surface or groundwater at a frequency or duration sufficient to support...a prevalence of vegetation typically adapted for life in saturated soil conditions." The line dividing wetlands from dry lands is not distinct but rather is shaded in gray, occurring across a continuum. In practical terms, readers who visit sites described in this book may find themselves canoeing a river swamp or hiking in its floodplain during drier times of the year. In either case, you do not necessarily have to get your feet wet. It helps, however, to be willing and prepared to do so. Getting your feet wet is part of the wetlands experience. Just ask any fisherman, birdwatcher, hiker, or hunter.

I've attempted to dispel some of the popular myths surrounding wetlands—namely that they are foul-smelling and forbidding places whose murky depths harbor disease and diabolical creatures. Nothing could be further from the truth. A healthy wetland teems with life, has some of the purest water found anywhere, and carries a light floral scent, if it smells at all. Wetlands provide habitat for rare and fascinating species of flora and fauna, including carnivorous plants that trap and devour insects, and wildlife ranging from the Day-Glo green Pine Barrens tree frog to the red-cockaded woodpecker, from manatees to whooping cranes, from blackside dace minnows to American crocodiles. Birds by the millions make wetlands their home all or part of the year, and annual migrations to places like Lake Mattamuskeet and Cape Romain are awesome in number, spectacle, and grandeur.

In addition, wetlands buffer ocean shorelines and offer flood protection along river corridors. They provide shelter as well as breeding and nursery grounds for a multitude of species, a fact that is especially evident along the coast, where salt marshes serve to seed ocean fisheries. Wetlands function as cleansing filters, removing pollutants from the water that passes through them. Wetlands recharge groundwater aquifers, preserving municipal water supplies. And wetlands also provide a broad spectrum of recreational activities.

The sites selected for writeups in the pages that follow represent a cross section of wetland types and a geographical distribution across five Southeastern states. A couple of other factors were important in considering sites. They had to be publicly accessible parks, forests, or refuges that offer enough in the way of recreational or educational opportunities to justify a visit. Each site has its own interesting combination of activities, with camping, hiking, canoeing, fishing, hunting, photography, and nature study principal among them.

Wetlands are remarkable places, and we hope that some of their beauty, uniqueness, and serenity shines through in the photographs and prose. We encourage readers to explore these sites and respectfully enjoy what they have to offer. We also urge you to be mindful of the great losses of wetlands that have occurred in this country since the mid-18th century and that are still going on today. Wetlands are precious and irreplaceable. They represent some of the last wild places where one can encounter nature in the raw, essentially untouched by civilization.

Wetlands deserve the utmost care and preservation. They also are places to be enjoyed. In the great spirit of the outdoors, lace up your sneakers, hiking boots, waders, or whatever footwear seems appropriate and explore some of our beautiful Southeastern wetlands.

— PARKE PUTERBAUGH
Greensboro, North Carolina

GEORGIA

Alcovy River Greenway

WETLANDS TYPES:

Piedmont river swamp, bottomland hardwoods

Quiet stretch of the Alcovy River
John Netherton

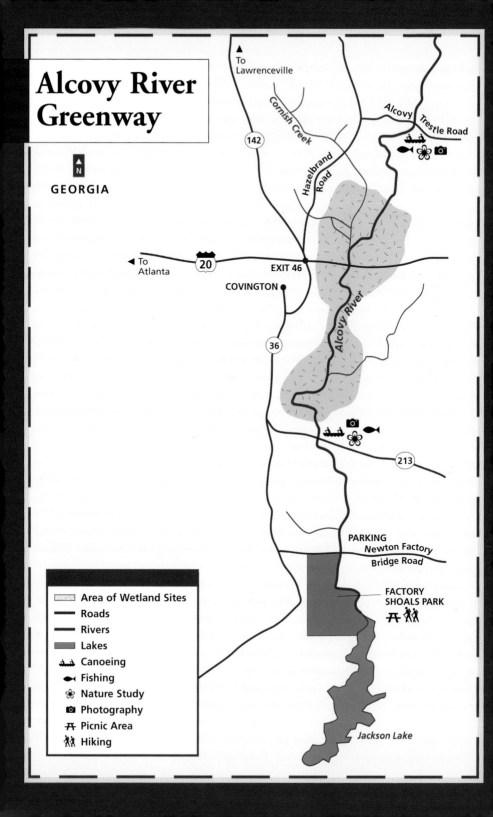

Alcovy River Greenway

GEORGIA

To Lawrenceville

142

Cornish Creek

Hazelbrand Road

Alcovy Trestle Road

To Atlanta

20

EXIT 46

COVINGTON

36

Alcovy River

213

PARKING
Newton Factory Bridge Road

FACTORY SHOALS PARK

Jackson Lake

Legend

- Area of Wetland Sites
- Roads
- Rivers
- Lakes
- Canoeing
- Fishing
- Nature Study
- Photography
- Picnic Area
- Hiking

ould you believe that not 30 miles from Atlanta, a city of three
million people, a pristine river flows through a peaceful backcountry of swamps and bottomlands? That this same river serves
as a corridor and sanctuary for an astounding variety of wildlife?
That this serene, meandering river with minimal rapids actually brought a
controversial river-control program to an end several decades ago? Meet the
Alcovy River.

Nothing about the Alcovy is typical. Although it flows through the
Piedmont region of Georgia, in some ways its flora and fauna more closely
resemble those found in a Coastal Plain swamp. For instance, one of the dominant tree species in the broad floodplain of the Alcovy is the water tupelo, or
tupelo gum. This graceful tree with a buttressed base stands clean and straight,
rising 80 to 90 feet to a narrow crown. Its purple, sour-pulped fruit is
devoured by birds and mammals when it ripens and drops in the autumn.
Like bald cypress, tupelos can live in standing water, but their seed cannot
germinate there. Instead, the fruit must wash onto a dry bank or bar in order
for germination to occur. The greenish-white flower of the tupelo provides
nectar for honeybees. The bees construct hives in tree cavities and produce
mild-tasting, much-prized tupelo honey.

Tupelo gums are commonly found on the Coastal Plain in association with bald cypress, but they are outside their range on the Piedmont Plateau.
Don't tell that to the Alcovy River, where dense, healthy stands of tupelo fill
its swamps with iridescent, filtered sunlight and stately quietude. More than
75 miles separate the tupelos of the Alcovy River from the nearest tupelo
population on the Coastal Plain. It has been theorized that the tupelo gum
swamp of the Alcovy is a relict—a biological island, in a sense—from a time
10,000 years ago when sea levels rose as glaciers retreated. What is now the
Piedmont was then the Coastal Plain. In effect, species like the tupelo gum,
the bird-voiced tree frog, and the mole salamander have been stranded along
the Alcovy in Newton County, creating isolated breeding populations. For
whatever reason, the Alcovy represents the northernmost extent of tupelos
into Georgia's Piedmont.

The Alcovy rises in Gwinnett County out of seepage bogs at Crowe
Lake, near the Atlanta suburb of Lawrenceville. It flows for roughly 80 miles
(44 miles as the crow flies) through Gwinnett, Walton, and Newton Counties,
emptying into Jackson Lake, an impoundment created by the Georgia Power
Company in 1911. The Alcovy is linked to another river, the Altamaha (see

Overleaf: Riffles and pools on the Alcovy River
John Netherton

separate entry), which drains the second largest watershed in the Southeast. The Alcovy is just a modest branch that eventually becomes part of the giant trunk known as the Altamaha. But its size and appearance can be deceiving. When push comes to shove, the Alcovy really packs a punch. In fact, it helped bring a misguided river-engineering program to its knees.

The story begins back in the 1950s, when the U.S. Soil Conservation Service (now the Natural Resources Conservation Service) and the Army Corps of Engineers began embarking on programs of river and stream channelization. Public Law 566 legally empowered the Corps to spend billions of dollars of federal money to straighten waterways, ostensibly to serve human ends such as flood control. When a watercourse is channelized, dredges, bulldozers, back hoes, and drag lines are used to deepen river bottoms, straighten river bends, flatten riverbanks, and eliminate islands. Trees and vegetation are stripped away for a hundred feet on both banks, leaving silty, denuded ditches through which water rushes swiftly. Although flood control was often a stated goal, holding back flood waters is considerably more difficult without floodplains. At the time, the government agencies had what they believed was a sound rationale. Now, the science of river morphology and the consequences of channelization projects tell us otherwise.

By the late 1960s, plans were afoot to channelize 2,000 miles of streams and rivers in Georgia's watersheds. Resistance to the proposed channelization of the Alcovy was launched by Georgia biologist and professor Charles Wharton, who spearheaded efforts to educate and mobilize the public. Mostly because of his persistence, concerned agencies and individuals took up the cause. State agencies like the Game and Fish Commission, environmental groups like the Georgia Wildlife Federation and Ducks Unlimited, and citizens who had grown up fishing, hunting, and combing the Alcovy River and its associated swamps and bottomlands raised a hue and cry.

Agencies unaccustomed to having their authority challenged were forced to back down as even congressmen joined calls to halt channelization. In March 1974, the Alcovy Watershed Project was abandoned on grounds that it was no longer economically feasible. In time, funding for Public Law 566 was deauthorized, and the federal subsidy of river channelization projects has subsequently been subjected to closer scrutiny. Today, new knowledge has been put to work in the service of watershed management and channel restoration and maintenance.

To visit the Alcovy is to explore a world that is relatively untouched by civilization, considering the river's proximity to Atlanta. In addition to the tupelos that tower over the standing water of the river swamp, numerous species of hardwoods thrive in the irregularly flooded bottomlands. Even minute changes in elevation affect the composition of tree species in swamps such as these, where bottomland hardwoods grow on sites that are inundated six months or less a year. River birch and green ash grow on the streambanks, their boughs overhanging the water and their trunks hosting an array of climbing vines. Within the bottomlands regime, species that are well-adapted to flooding include sweetgum, overcup oak, and red maple. On better drained terraces, beech, swamp chestnut oak, loblolly pine, and bitternut hickory are found. Water oak, green ash, and pawpaw trees inhabit more thoroughly drained sandy loams. Still farther upland, drier ridges support red and white oaks, dogwood trees, and hawthorn bushes.

Among all of them, the pawpaw has the greatest natural and historical association with the region. It is believed the very name "Alcovy" was derived from the Muscogee Indian word for pawpaw. They named the river Ulcofauhatchie, which combines the Muscogee words for pawpaw (*ulcofau*) and river (*hatchie*). Over the centuries, "Ulcofau" was amended to "Alcovy."

The fruit of the pawpaw is devoured by birds and mammals. Humans also have been known to consume it. In the past, Southerners would bake its

Canopy-covered section of the Alcovy River, by John Netherton

21

sweet yellow pulp into pies. More promising are preliminary indications that the bark of the pawpaw contains a chemical called asimicin, which acts as a natural pesticide. Its twigs and small branches also may harbor a potent anti-cancer agent. Two species of this understory tree are found along the Alcovy. A pawpaw can be easily identified by its leaves, which give off an aroma like bell pepper. The fruit of the pawpaw barely ripens before practically every creature in the forest, people included, tries to make off with it.

Like most Georgia rivers, the Alcovy moves somewhat mysteriously across the landscape, concealing itself like a slithering snake. It is crossed only infrequently by bridges and even then is hidden beneath tunnels of overhanging greenery. As yet, access to the river is limited, as are activities that can be done on it. Enterprising canoeists can paddle the river. (Come prepared for plentiful snags, necessitating frequent portages.) There are put-ins where Alcovy Trestle Road and GA 213 cross the Alcovy. The river can be canoed from either launch site down to Factory Shoals Park, a county-run park at the north end of Jackson Lake. If you put in at Alcovy Trestle Road, expect a full day of canoeing, during which you will stay as wet as a river cooter. The trip from GA 213 is shorter and easier. At Factory Shoals Park, you can picnic on the banks of Jackson Lake, among other activities.

Although it survived the channelization threat, the Alcovy presently is at risk from pollution and habitat loss, as industry and development advance upon it. The Alcovy River Greenway Project, a joint undertaking of the Georgia Wildlife Federation and the Conservation Fund, was launched in 1993 to raise awareness of the river's plight and to develop a protective greenway along the Alcovy. Thus far, fundraising efforts have resulted in the purchase of 200 highly sensitive acres of river swamp. Outreach efforts have won cooperation from private landowners in the form of conservation easements and voluntary inclusion in a land registry.

Long-range plans include construction of the Alcovy Environmental Education Center. Its mission will be "to provide quality education and training opportunities for those leaders who will deliver the environmental message to the next generation." The center will be sited near the Alcovy in order to provide everyone, from schoolchildren to public officials, the opportunity to learn about the Alcovy River in particular and wetlands environments in general. The state headquarters of the Georgia Wildlife Federation will be sited there as well.

With such programs being supported by an increasingly involved public, the Alcovy and riverine wetlands throughout the Southeast may well continue to function as water purifiers, flood-storage basins, rechargers of groundwater aquifers, repositories of uniquely adapted trees and enchanting sights, and laboratories in which a mind-boggling variety of flora and fauna reproduce and flourish while being studied by respectful human caretakers.

LOCATION The Alcovy River, from its headwaters near Lawrenceville, flows for 80 miles into Jackson Lake in Newton County. The river is accessible to canoeists at two put-in points. One is located north of Covington. From I-20, take Exit 46 and head north on GA 142. Turn right on Hazelbrand Road and right again on Alcovy Trestle Road. The boat launch is located where the road crosses the river. The other site, located farther downstream, can be reached by taking GA 36 south from Covington to GA 213 east. Put in where GA 213 crosses the Alcovy. The Alcovy empties into Jackson Lake at Factory Shoals Park, which is reachable by taking GA 36 south from Covington, turning east on Newton Factory Bridge Road, and then following signs to the park.

WHEN IT'S OPEN Most of the land in the Alcovy River Greenway is private property and is therefore inaccessible to the public. Construction of the Alcovy Environmental Education Center and its demonstration gardens and trails are still in the planning stages. Currently, occasional seminars and events are held in the Turner Alcovy Cabin, a restored log cabin that sits on a parcel of land abutting the Alcovy River and is owned by the Georgia Wildlife Federation. For information on such events and how to get involved in the Alcovy River Project, contact the Georgia Wildlife Federation (see address below).

BEST TIMES TO VISIT Canoeing is best in spring when the water levels are elevated. It is easier to explore the floodplain on foot at other times of year, especially in late summer and early fall when water levels are down in the swamp.

WHAT TO DO Canoeing, fishing, photography, nature study, picnicking, and hiking.

WHERE TO STAY Accommodations are available in Covington, 30 miles east of Atlanta on I-20.

FOR MORE INFORMATION Alcovy River Greenway, c/o Georgia Wildlife Federation, 1930 Iris Drive, Conyers, GA 30207 (770-929-3350).

GEORGIA

Altamaha River Bioreserve

WETLANDS TYPES:

Bottomland hardwoods, cypress swamp, isolated wetlands,
freshwater and salt marshes

Cypress trees within the Altamaha floodplain
John Netherton

hat is a bioreserve? Here is a definition provided by The Nature Conservancy: "A bioreserve is a landscape, usually large in size, with naturally functioning ecological processes, containing outstanding examples of ecosystems, natural communities, and species that are endangered or inadequately protected." The bioreserve concept involves brokering cooperative agreements among private landowners, large corporations, small businesses, state and federal agencies, and conservation groups. Such a multiagency, partnership-oriented, systemwide conservation plan has been drawn up and is being implemented along the Altamaha River.

The Nature Conservancy has been active in the lower watershed of the Altamaha as far back as 1969, when it helped acquire a couple of islands in the river's mouth for inclusion in the chain of Savannah National Wildlife Refuges. The bioreserve approach emerged in the early 1990s, promising to become a significant new strategy for environmental management. The Nature Conservancy has for decades acquired tracts of environmentally sensitive lands and then set them aside as preserves or turned them over to government agencies. It is taking a somewhat different tack with projects like the Altamaha and South Carolina's ACE Basin (see separate entry) that has less to do with purchasing land than with educating and working with landowners and obtaining conservation easements. Within the Altamaha River Bioreserve— an area occupying 1.2 million acres—The Nature Conservancy owns two tracts totaling 1,119 acres. Only ten percent of the bioreserve is in the hands of state and federal agencies. The new thinking is that private ownership, economic sustainability, and ecosystem health can all coexist.

The lower Altamaha River, its floodplain, and delta are significant for several reasons. Most important, the Altamaha River basin is the second largest watershed on the East Coast. It also has the second highest flow rate of any Eastern river, emptying more than 100,000 cubic feet per second into the Atlantic Ocean. It drains 14,000 square miles of Piedmont and Coastal Plain—roughly one-fourth of the state of Georgia. Moreover, the Altamaha River—from the confluence of the rivers that form it to the Atlantic Ocean —has never been dammed or channelized. In other words, its hydrology remains essentially unaltered by human engineering.

The basin harbors over 125 rare or endangered plant and animal species, including 4 that are ranked G1 (globally imperiled): the Georgia spiny mussel (*Elliptio spinosa*), Radford's dicerandra or Radford's balm (*Dicerandra radfordiana*), hairy rattleweed (*Bapitista arachnifera*), and Alabama milkvine (*Matelea alabamensis*). Six species of pearly mussels found on the Altamaha exist nowhere else in the world. Then there is the

Franklinia (*Gordonia alatamaha*), one of the most historically interesting floristic species in the Southeast. Originally discovered along the Altamaha River in 1765, it was last seen in 1790. Botanists are still searching the wilds for the lost *Gordonia*. It has, however, been perpetuated in cultivation.

The Altamaha River is formed by the confluence of the Oconee and Ocmulgee Rivers in middle Georgia. The Altamaha is further fed by the Ohoopee River and numerous tributary creeks. The river winds its way across the lower Coastal Plain for 137 miles (89 miles as the crow flies). It is crossed only six times in 137 miles: by five highways and one active railroad bridge. Although it passes through largely pristine country, the Altamaha has state prison, a nuclear plant, and a pulp-and-paper mill situated on its banks. The river forms a broad, fan-shaped delta as it approaches the coast, depositing an enormous sediment load as it slows. As sediment drops out, it forms islands within the river's mouth and also feeds the barrier islands along the Georgia coast as it is reworked by long-shore currents. A variety of wetlands exists within the river basin, including floodplain swamps, salt marshes, isolated wetlands, and reclaimed rice paddies now used for waterfowl management.

The multijurisdictional approach has resulted in a mosaic of public lands scattered up and down the river. (It is worth remembering that more than 90 percent of the land within the Altamaha River Bioreserve remains in private hands.) The principal title holder to public land in the Altamaha Basin is the Georgia Department of Natural Resources, which maintains five Wildlife Management Areas (WMAs) on the river. These WMAs provide the best way to explore the river basin, save for being on the river itself in a canoe or motorboat. Following are summaries of the five WMAs along the Altamaha, beginning at the river's mouth and moving upstream:

Altamaha Waterfowl Management Area—The largest of all WMA tracts within the Altamaha River basin, this 26,000-acre area includes land in and around the river's mouth near Darien and upriver for ten miles to a crossroads named Cox. The most readily accessible area is Champney Island. The turnoff to the Champney Island Interpretive Trail is on U.S. 17, between the bridges that span the Champney and South Altamaha Rivers, just south of Darien. The mile-long trail follows the perimeter of the Champney Island waterfowl impoundment, a restored marsh that occupies the site of what used to be a rice paddy. The rice planters' old diking system, dating from the 1880s, is now used for managing growth of the aquatic grasses waterfowl need for food and habitat. While walking, you will see turtles scooting off the banks and startle flapping waterbirds off the pond. Tread softly and pause to listen and observe. One large field is managed as a habitat for snipe, a

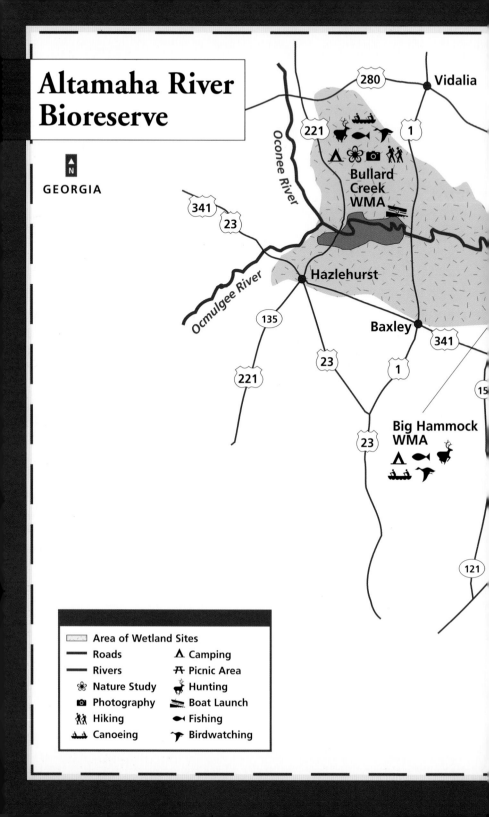

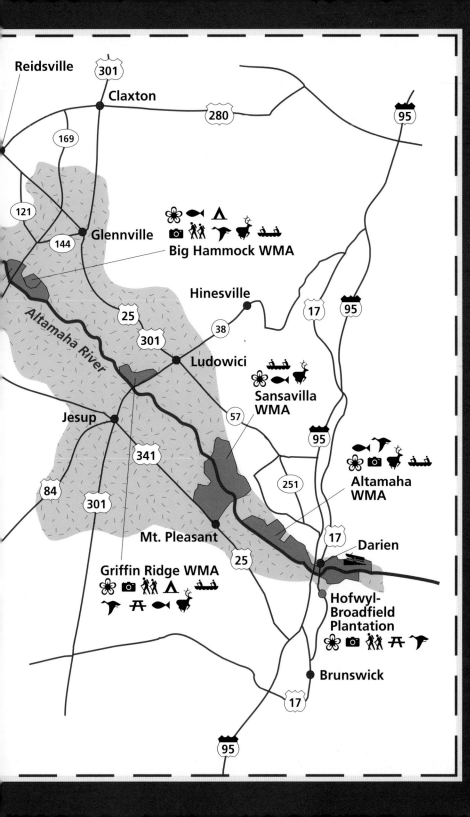

Reidsville

301

Claxton

280

95

169

121

144

Glennville

Big Hammock WMA

Hinesville

25

301

Ludowici

38

17

95

Altamaha River

Jesup

341

57

Sansavilla
WMA

95

84

301

251

Altamaha
WMA

Mt. Pleasant

25

17

Darien

Griffin Ridge WMA

Hofwyl-
Broadfield
Plantation

Brunswick

17

95

marsh bird that pokes around mud flats for insect larvae. Wood ducks use manmade nesting boxes that have been erected. In any given year, 90 percent of the nesting boxes within the Altamaha WMA are occupied by "woodies" that return to the same boxes year after year. Many species of wading birds, shorebirds, and dabbling and diving ducks can be seen from the trail and the observation tower at the trailhead. Directly across U.S. 17 is a large parking lot and public boat launch. While in the area, you also can take the Altamaha Byway, an 11-mile driving tour of historic and natural sites in the delta of the Altamaha along U.S. 17. Historic sites along the byway include Fort King George (an earthen fort that was the British Empire's southern outpost in North America) and Hofwyl-Broadfield Plantation (a restored antebellum rice plantation and state historic site along the Altamaha).

The tidal influence of the ocean extends far upriver, but the location that demarcates brackish and freshwater along the Altamaha is at the I-95 bridge crossing. West of the interstate, you will need a freshwater fishing license to drop a line in the river. Fishing expeditions can be launched from landings along the length of the river. Five fish camps offer camping, bait and tackle, food, and fuel. Four of the five camps rent boats, while Adamson's Fish Camp also rents cabins and serves some of the best catfish chowder in Georgia. For a listing of fish camps and 21 other launch points along the river, contact the Game and Fish Division of the Georgia Department of Natural Resources (205 Butler Street SE, Suite 1358, Atlanta, GA 30334). Request the brochure entitled *Guide to Fishing the Altamaha River*. Those in the know talk reverently of Ebenezer Bend, a bend in the river where the water is deep and the fishing is unsurpassed.

Another point of entry into the Altamaha WMA can be found near Cox. To get there, take GA 251 west from Darien. Three miles west of I-95, where the road forks, bear left and then turn left again by the railroad over-pass at Cox. At this point, you probably will see more turtles crossing the road than cars whizzing down it. The paved road turns to gravel and then to deep sand. From the gates of the WMA, you can park and walk toward the river, crossing ridges and fording sloughs. It is a guaranteed adventure for those who know what they are doing. Carry a compass and the relevant USGS quadrangle maps. (For maps call the U.S. Geological Survey Earth Science Information Center in Reston, Virginia, at 1-800-872-6277.) This upper portion of the WMA, known as Lewis Island Natural Area, includes virgin cypress stands deep in its interior. There are guides for hire in the area; inquire at local fish camps for names and telephone numbers.

Previous page: Freshwater marsh at Altamaha Waterfowl Management Area
John Netherton

Green heron, by John Netherton

Sansavilla Wildlife Management Area—This 17,800-acre WMA lies between the town of Mount Pleasant and the Altamaha River, approximately 20 miles northwest of Brunswick off U.S. 25/341. Straddling Wayne and Glynn Counties, it is primarily managed for small game, deer, and turkey hunting. As with all WMAs, if you are not here to hunt, make sure you know when the various seasons open and close for your own safety. A small park, Altamaha Park, lies at the end of County Road 581, beside a railroad bridge over the river. This area also is of historical interest because an early settlement was located on the bluffs above the river.

Griffin Ridge Wildlife Management Area—Get out your funkiest pair of hiking boots, because you will likely wind up ankle deep in mud on the hiking trails that run through this 5,616-acre WMA located off U.S. 25/301 between Jesup and Ludowici. At this point, the floodplain of the Altamaha is five miles wide. Bridges cross over massive cypress swamps and bottomland hardwoods that extend north of the river. The Griffin Ridge WMA is situated on a sand ridge, and its trails run along the edge of the swamp. The best hiking is along the south flank of Griffin Ridge. Coming north from Jesup on U.S. 25/301, turn left at the first of two entrances into the WMA. A trail crosses the dirt road through the WMA near the second parking lot. It follows the edge of the swamp for a good distance. You will be rewarded with the unearthly spectacle of giant cypress standing in still, milky-brown water. Hardwoods occupy the irregularly flooded sites where the sand ridge and alluvial swamp meet. This is perhaps the best way to glimpse the generally inaccessible floodplain of the Altamaha.

***Big Hammock Public Fishing Area and Wildlife Management
Area and Big Hammock Natural Area***—Big Hammock occupies 6,400 acres
of bottomland hardwood forest on the floodplain of the Altamaha River, just
north of the bridge that is crossed by GA 121/144/169. The closest town is
Glennville, 12 miles northeast via GA 144. The bridge is a prime vantage point
for a glimpse of this rarely crossed and often hidden river. Big Hammock is
a fine place to fish, hike, hunt, birdwatch, and study various lowland forest
communities in close proximity: turkey oak/longleaf pine forest, cypress/gum
swamp forest, and a big hammock forest dominated by hydric (water-loving)
broadleaf evergreens. Big Hammock also provides a habitat for the rare Georgia
plume (*Elliottia racemosa*). Trails and roads snake through Big Hammock
PFA/WMA and Big Hammock Natural Area, which adjoin one another.
Access may be limited in wet weather or high-water stages. The period of
peak discharge is late January through early April. The best time to come is
late summer, when the waters have receded and the floodplain has dried out.
September and October are the height of hunting season, so wear a blaze
orange cap and vest. Easiest access into Big Hammock is via the entrance
road off GA 121/144/169, just north of the bridge (look for a sign). Be
aware that the bumpy, sandy roads at Big Hammock may be hard on a small
car's suspension. Four-wheel-drive vehicles or two feet are the preferred
modes of getting around. Obtain a map of the area from the Georgia
Department of Natural Resources if you plan on visiting Big Hammock; it
is a veritable maze.

Bullard Creek Wildlife Management Area—This 13,000-acre
WMA runs from the confluence of the Ocmulgee and Oconee Rivers, whose
union creates the Altamaha, east almost to the U.S. 1 bridge. At the west end,
access roads inside the WMA come close to the point where the rivers meet.
But Bullard Creek WMA mainly exists—as do all WMAs, for the most part
—as hunting grounds. It is not an ideal way to get close to the Altamaha
and its wetlands, but it is about the only way—unless, of course, you take a
canoe or boat out on the river, spending nights at fish camps along the way.

A drive up the Altamaha, from its mouth to its headwaters, making
detours into a WMA or two for a look at the landscape, makes a pleasant day
trip. You can also do some antiquing or buy farmers' produce at stands along
the way. For a scenic drive through rural Georgia that crosses the river twice,
take U.S. 25/341 from Brunswick to Jesup, and then cross the Altamaha via
U.S. 25/301 en route to Ludowici. Continue to Glennville, picking up GA
144 west until it meets GA 121/169 and crosses the river again. To complete
the circuit, return to Brunswick via U.S. 341.

While you are in Brunswick, be sure to visit the extensive salt marshes that inspired poet Sidney Lanier to compose the celebrated poem of tribute "The Marshes of Glynn" while sitting beneath an oak tree viewing his beloved "golden isles." For those desiring a complete coastal wetlands experience, trips can be made by passenger ferry to Sapelo Island (north of Darien) and Cumberland Island (south of Brunswick). The entire lower Coastal Plain of southeast Georgia, one soon comes to realize, is an endless wetland of golden marshes and hidden rivers.

LOCATION   The Altamaha River flows for 137 miles across southeast Georgia, entering the ocean near Darien. When you are traveling upriver from its mouth, the Altamaha WMA is located on and around the river delta near Darien, including the Champney Island site, which is off U.S. 17 between Darien and Brunswick. Sansavilla WMA is entered via Sansavilla Road, off U.S. 25/341 in Mount Pleasant, 13 miles southeast of Jesup. Griffin Ridge WMA is located between Jesup and Ludowici on U.S. 25/301. Big Hammock PFA/WMA is roughly 20 miles northwest of Jesup and is entered by turning from GA 121/144/169 onto Big Hammock Road or County Road 441, just north of the bridge over the Altamaha. Bullard Creek WMA is located where the Altamaha begins, at the confluence of the Oconee and Ocmulgee Rivers, 20 miles south of Vidalia off U.S. 221/GA 135.

WHEN IT'S OPEN   Public lands maintained by the Georgia Department of Natural Resources, including various Waterfowl and Wildlife Management Areas, are open from sunup to sundown.

BEST TIMES TO VISIT   Fall is prime hunting season on the state Wildlife Management Areas along the Altamaha. For a schedule of seasons for various game animals, write the Georgia Department of Natural Resources, Game and Fish Division, Suite 1358-Floyd Towers East, 205 Butler Street SE, Atlanta, GA 30334.

WHAT TO DO   Fishing, hunting, canoeing, hiking, and nature study.

WHERE TO STAY   In addition to a few small motels in Darien, accommodations are available in nearby Brunswick and at the coastal resorts on St. Simons and Jekyll Islands. Camping is available at Griffin Ridge, Bullard Creek, and Big Hammock WMAs. Cabins are available on the Altamaha River at Adamson's Fish Camp (912-654-3632).

FOR MORE INFORMATION   Altamaha River Bioreserve, The Nature Conservancy of Georgia, P.O. Box 484, Darien, GA 31305 (912-437-2161).

GEORGIA

Chattooga River

WETLANDS TYPES:
Minerotrophic bogs, riverine wetlands, beaver ponds,
headwater springs, mountain coves

Bog at Russell Bridge
John Netherton

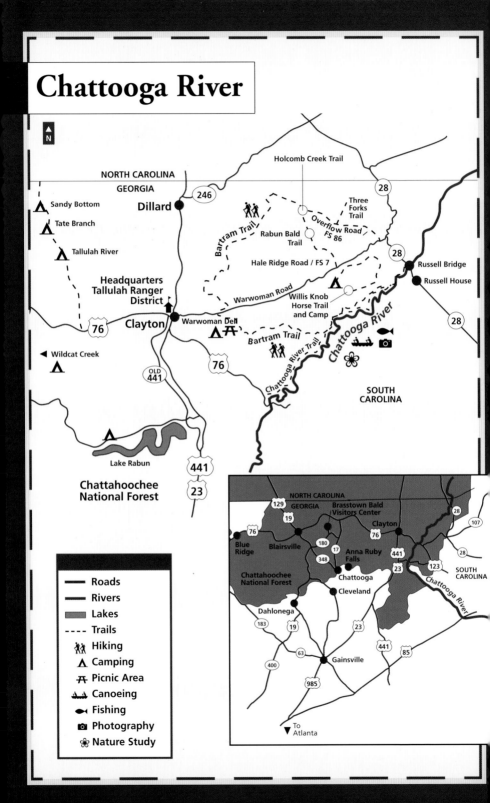

Chattooga River

N

NORTH CAROLINA
GEORGIA

Sandy Bottom
Tate Branch
Tallulah River

Dillard

246

Holcomb Creek Trail

Bartram Trail

Rabun Bald Trail

Three Forks Trail

Overflow Road FS 86

28

28

Russell Bridge
Russell House

Hale Ridge Road / FS 7

Headquarters
Tallulah Ranger
District

Warwoman Road

Willis Knob
Horse Trail
and Camp

Chattooga River

76

Clayton

Warwoman Dell

Bartram Trail

Chattooga River Trail

28

Wildcat Creek

76

SOUTH
CAROLINA

OLD
441

Lake Rabun

441

Chattahoochee
National Forest

23

NORTH CAROLINA
GEORGIA

129

Brasstown Bald
Visitors Center

Clayton

28

107

76

19

Blue
Ridge

Blairsville

180

17

Anna Ruby
Falls

76

441

28

348

123

SOUTH
CAROLINA

Chattooga

Chattahoochee
National Forest

Cleveland

23

Chattooga River

Dahlonega

183

19

23

441

85

63

Gainsville

400

985

To
Atlanta

Legend

— Roads
— Rivers
▬ Lakes
---- Trails
🥾 Hiking
⛺ Camping
⛱ Picnic Area
🛶 Canoeing
🎣 Fishing
📷 Photography
❀ Nature Study

Generally, in terms of area, there are not as many wetlands at higher elevations as can be found on the Piedmont and Coastal Plains. One reason is that many mountain wetlands have been extensively altered by agriculture because these "bottoms" are easily accessible and productive. Then, there is the matter of drainage patterns, which are radically different in mountainous regions where fast-moving creeks and streams do not have wide, well-developed floodplains. Yet wetland sites do exist in the mountains of north Georgia and in the neighboring states of North and South Carolina. These wetlands are relatively rare in occurrence and limited in size—again, largely due to historical losses, having been drained and destroyed to make way for farming and human settlements. But they are unmistakably wetlands, unique and notable for the communities they support.

Within Georgia's 750,000-acre Chattahoochee National Forest and along the Chattooga River in particular, one can ferret out an intriguing handful of wetlands. This is a land of many waterfalls, moist mountain coves, and abundant precipitation—as much as 80 to100 inches in places. The north Georgia mountains receive the most precipitation of any site in the state and some of the highest annual rainfall averages in the eastern United States. The Chattahoochee is a land brimming with recreational opportunities, including challenging whitewater rafting on the Chattooga, dramatic waterfalls and mountains, superb trout fishing, and an extensive system of hiking trails. The national forest is crossed by 830 miles of trails, including the following major backpacker routes: the Appalachian Trail (79 miles of which passes through here), Bartram Trail (37 miles), Benton Mackaye Trail (53 miles), Duncan Ridge Trail (53 miles), and Chattooga River Trail (10 miles).

Because the Chattahoochee National Forest is so extensive, this discussion will focus on sites in the Tallulah Ranger District, possibly the most scenic of the eight districts. The Tallulah Ranger District is headquartered in Clayton, Georgia, a charming small town and provisioning center that serves as a starting point and place to stay for many visitors. Clayton lies at the heart of Rabun County, which is essentially one big parkland. (Interestingly and somewhat sadly, the town itself was built on a floodplain and former wetlands, and it experiences significant flooding problems as a result.) Of the county's 377 square miles, 63 percent belong to the U.S. Forest Service. In addition, Rabun County boasts three state parks, including Georgia's highest (Black Rock Mountain, which lies astride the eastern Continental Divide at 3,640 feet) and deepest (Tallulah Gorge State Park, whose chasm plunges 1,000 feet).

The first stop on this wetlands tour is where GA 28 crosses the Chattooga River at Russell Bridge. The west side of the bridge provides an entrée, via a short, overgrown footpath at the head of a small parking lot, to a five-acre bog. In contrast to the classic Appalachian mountain bogs, which are highly acidic, organic-rich, and mineral-poor (see Blanton Forest entry), the soil at the Russell Bridge bog is minerotrophic—alkaline in chemistry and rich in minerals. The bog occupies an oval depression at the foot of Alf Hill on the west bank of the Chattooga, just above its confluence with the West Fork. Formerly, the site was an old cornfield that reverted to wetlands after the Chattooga was designated a Wild and Scenic River. Perhaps the last thing one might expect to find on a river renowned for its Class 4, 5, and 6 rapids is a sedentary bog off to one side. But between Russell Bridge and Earls Ford—a distance of seven miles—the Chattooga's flow is relatively calm.

The short trail that leads to the edge of the bog is an obstacle course, including switchcane among its tangle. The bog itself has no overstory. Islands of shrublike speckled alder, commonly found in wet thickets, occupy a basin full of standing water that is covered chest-high with sedges and rushes. Jewelweed and arrowhead—the former an orange-yellow wildflower, the latter an emergent aquatic herb with distinctive arrow-shaped leaves— are among the profusion of plants that thrive in the bog. Red maple and American holly stand along the raised perimeter. A proper inventory of the flora and fauna at this site has not been made, nor has its hydrology been studied. However, the Russell Bridge bog resembles two well-studied minerotrophic bogs in the North Carolina mountains: Standing Indian Bog, which forms the headwaters of the Nantahala River and lies below the campground of the same name, and Horse Cove Bog, which lies east of Highlands at the confluence of Edwards Creek and Black Rock Branch.

Across GA 28 from the Russell Bridge parking lot, hikers can pick up the Bartram Trail, which runs south along the Chattooga for a quarter mile before turning up the West Fork for a short distance. At this point, a wet ford of the river is necessary before the trail resumes its southward course along the Chattooga. The portion of trail that skirts the riverbanks before crossing the West Fork follows a narrow band of riverine wetlands. Water-tolerant plants thrive on the river's moist and occasionally flooded banks. Bring along a field guide to wetlands herbs, shrubs, and wildflowers, and see how many you can identify. You might be surprised!

The next stop is Ammons Creek and Holcomb Falls—north Georgia's most stunning set of waterfalls. The trailhead lies 21 miles from Clayton, and the drive to it includes 7 miles of gravel Forest Service roads. Rest assured the sights are well worth the effort it takes to get there. Holcomb Creek Trail is a splendid three-mile loop that passes through scenic, wooded high country. The surrounding forest holds excellent second-growth stands of white pine, Eastern hemlock, and yellow poplar, all of which do well in the moist coves and on the hillsides of the southern Blue Ridge. The streambanks are covered with mountain laurel and white rhododendron, flowering favorites of high-country visitors. Downed trees returning to soil wear a thick carpet of moss and fungi on their backs. Ferns thrive in these damp environs. The fragrant air is filled with the sounds of bird calls and cascading water.

The trail reaches Holcomb Creek Falls first. Mist hangs in the air as the creek tumbles in a roaring descent for 120 feet. Rhododendron growing out of a giant, fallen hemlock are constantly bathed in the torrent. Farther up the trail, an observation deck provides an intimate encounter with Ammons Creek Falls, a cataract that roars over fallen trunks and limbs that have become trapped by boulders in the current. Incidentally, Holcomb Creek and Ammons Creek Falls are just two of eight notable waterfalls in the Tallulah Ranger District. The others are Angel, Panther, Becky Branch, Martin Creek, Minnehaha, and Dicks Creek Falls. A printed handout detailing waterfalls and directions can be obtained at the Chattahoochee National Forest Visitor Center in Clayton.

Broad-winged damselfly, by John Netherton

The last stops on this brief tour of waterfalls and wetlands near Clayton have both history and natural features to commend them. Russell House, located on the South Carolina side of the Chattooga River (which serves as the state line), is a historic structure that was a working inn during the 1800s. Travelers would stay there when the Chattooga was too deep to cross. Three buildings stood on the site, although the inn itself was burned to the ground by vandals in recent years and only the chimney remains standing. A spring house and active springs still exist on the property. On the site are clusters of royal fern. Commonly found in wet springhead areas, this junglelike fern can reach six feet in height. Tall stands of jewelweed run along the watercourse. Also known as touch-me-nots, they expel seeds from capsules with a force that disperses them four feet or more. Another interesting herb that grows among the spring-fed thickets at Russell House is joe-pye-weed, a family of wetlands-loving plants whose pink flowers attract butterflies. This is just a sample of the hydric herbs and wildflowers found around the springheads at Russell House.

Finally, no visit to the area is complete without a picnic at Warwoman Dell. History is evident in the surviving handiwork of the Civilian Conservation Corps, which built the pavilion, picnic tables, and trout ponds during the Depression. Botanist and traveler William Bartram passed through here while making field trips in the late 18th century. The trail that bears his name crosses Warwoman Dell today. Vegetation includes species commonly found along the banks of streams and in moist cove settings in the mountains of the Southeast. American sycamores and beeches grow along the streambanks. But the dominant species are Eastern hemlock and white pine, which favor cool, moist sites like Warwoman Dell. Rhododendron grow in dense thickets, their leaves and twig ends serving as forage for deer in winter. Other plants found along the banks of Warwoman Creek include sweet pepperbush, with its fragrant and attractive pale blossoms, and yellowroot, a shrub whose inner bark provides a folk remedy for indigestion.

Of course, one of the main attractions in Rabun County is white-water rafting on the Chattooga River. Just be sure to visit some of the wetlands sites that are found along the same rivers and streams. You will not regret it!

LOCATION The visitor center and headquarters for the Tallulah Ranger District of the Chattahoochee National Forest is located in Clayton on U.S. 441, just south of the intersection with U.S. 76. The Russell Bridge bog is located on GA 28 and the Chattooga River, approximately 20 miles east of Clayton. Russell House is located a few more miles down GA 28, on the South

Carolina side. Holcomb Creek Trail can be reached by driving 14 miles east of Clayton on Warwoman Road, then turning left on Overflow Road and proceeding 7 miles to its intersection with Hale Ridge Road. Warwoman Dell is located 4 miles east of Clayton on Warwoman Road.

WHEN IT'S OPEN The visitor center and headquarters for the Tallulah Ranger District is open Monday through Friday, 8:00 a.m. to 4:30 p.m. The center is also open on weekends from about mid-May until the end of October. But the hours of operation may vary from year to year. Check with the Tallulah Ranger District for campground schedules; most campgrounds are closed in winter.

BEST TIMES TO VISIT Spring thaws bring high water levels to the Chattooga River, resulting in the most challenging whitewater rafting. Water levels are lower in summer and fall, making for more relaxing float trips. Fall colors in the Chattahoochee National Forest are as dramatic as any in the East.

WHAT TO DO Canoeing, rafting, kayaking, camping, hiking, fishing, hunting, photography, and nature study. Three outfitters offer guided rafting trips on the Chattooga. They are the Nantahala Outdoor Center (800-232-7238), Wild Water Rafting (800-451-9972), and Southeastern Expeditions (800-868-7238).

WHERE TO STAY Campgrounds in the Tallulah Ranger District include the following: 80 sites on Lake Rabun, 48 sites on the Tallulah River, and 32 sites on Wildcat Creek. The town of Clayton has several hotels and motels, including the historic, restored Old Clayton Inn (706-782-7722) and the Shoneys Inn (706-782-2214). The latter is located across U.S. 441 from the visitor center and headquarters for the Tallulah Ranger District.

FOR MORE INFORMATION Tallulah Ranger District, Chattahoochee National Forest, U.S. 441 South, P.O. Box 438, Clayton, GA 30525 (706-782-3320). In addition, there are many fine travel guidebooks to the region, including the Georgia Conservancy's *Guide to the North Georgia Mountains*.

GEORGIA

Okefenokee Swamp

WETLANDS TYPES:

Gum-cypress swamp, prairie marsh, peat bogs

American alligator
John Netherton

L ike many wetlands, the Okefenokee Swamp sometimes suffers an undeservedly bad reputation. Travelers heading to or from Florida along I-95 assume that the sickly "rotten egg" odor permeating the air originates inside this massive, 600-square-mile swamp, which occupies much of the southeast corner of Georgia. Contrary to popular belief, the foul aroma that causes travelers to grimace is not the Okefenokee—which lies 25 miles west of I-95—but the paper mills and chemical plants of Brunswick, Woodbine, and St. Mary's, Georgia. The swamp itself has no discernible odor. The air and water are extraordinarily pure and fresh. A self-contained watershed that serves as a haven for a fascinating array of plants and animals, the Okefenokee is one of the most unexpectedly delightful environments in the Deep South.

It is well worth a detour from the main highway to experience this vast and mysterious wetland. In terms of name recognition, it is the most famous swamp in America. While everyone knows the name Okefenokee—an Indian term that translates as "land of trembling earth"—relatively few have bothered to visit. The saucer-shaped Okefenokee Swamp consists of cypress-studded open water, manmade canals, forested islands, alligator-filled ponds and lakes, and marshy, grass-covered prairies. There are no roads across it and only three points of entry along its perimeter:

East Entrance—gateway to the Okefenokee National Wildlife Refuge, near Folkston.

North Entrance—site of Okefenokee Swamp Park, a privately run, nonprofit sightseeing and educational park near Waycross.

West Entrance—leads to Stephen C. Foster State Park, a small park contained within the Okefenokee National Wildlife Refuge, near Fargo.

Opportunities for camping, hiking, canoeing, and more exist at all three entrances. A boat trip through the swamp, with or without a guide, is the best way to see the Okefenokee. Options range from an introductory, hour-long guided motorboat tour to a five-night, self-guided wilderness experience.

One thing that immediately stands out about the swamp is the color of the water. Viewed from a boat or dry land, the swamp appears clear and brown, like brewed tea or cola. It is tinted by tannins from the decomposing plant matter. Dip a glass or jug into the swamp and the water looks much lighter, almost like apple juice. Although it looks dirty, swamp water is pure and clean. In prior centuries, sailing ships would stock up on Okefenokee swamp water for use during transatlantic crossings. It was the only freshwater in the area that would not turn bad during a long voyage. More than 80 percent of the water in the swamp enters as rainfall, so the Okefenokee is

Palmetto and longleaf pine on Billy's Island, by John Netherton

not subject to pollution from incoming creeks and rivers. However, it is subject to air pollution and runoff from surrounding lands.

The hydrology of the Okefenokee Swamp is singularly fascinating. The swamp occupies a "perched basin" elevated above the surrounding landscape (imagine a saucer set on a table). The geological feature responsible for creating the swamp is Trail Ridge—a relict sandbar formed a million years ago when the Atlantic Ocean extended much farther inland. After the ocean receded to its present location, Trail Ridge acted as a dike, the basin behind it gradually filling with freshwater. Over time, plant life invaded the basin from the margins, and peat accumulated on the basin floor.

Peat deposition is due to incomplete decay of plant matter. Long growing seasons, brief winters, and extended periods of saturation are contributing factors. Organic matter is produced at a high rate, but it does not break down nearly as fast as it is created because the waterlogged soil contains little oxygen, which is necessary for its breakdown. The high acidity of humates leached from swamp vegetation further retards decomposition. Organic-rich, nutrient-poor peat beds have accumulated to depths of 15 feet in the Okefenokee. Occasionally, eruptions of gas from beneath the surface dislodge chunks of peat. These "peat blowups" result in floating islands that serve as substrates for grasses, shrubs, trees, and even animals. The Jell-O-like quality of these spongy, saturated peatlands led Native Americans to call them the "land of trembling earth."

Why, you might wonder, does the basin not fill in as the peat accumulates? The answer is fire. The Okefenokee Swamp is a fire-maintained

47

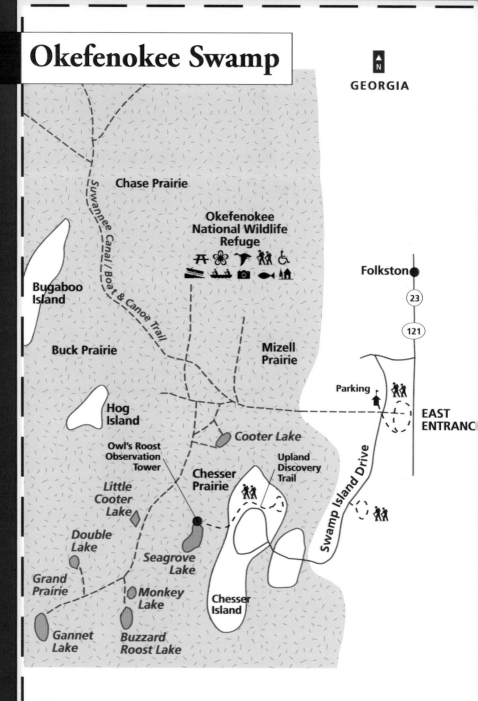

Okefenokee Swamp

N
GEORGIA

Chase Prairie

Okefenokee
National Wildlife
Refuge

Suwannee Canal / Boat & Canoe Trail

Bugaboo
Island

Buck Prairie

Folkston

23

121

Mizell
Prairie

Parking

Hog
Island

EAST
ENTRANCE

Cooter Lake

Owl's Roost
Observation
Tower

Upland
Discovery
Trail

Chesser
Prairie

Little
Cooter
Lake

Swamp Island Drive

Double
Lake

Seagrove
Lake

Grand
Prairie

Monkey
Lake

Chesser
Island

Gannet
Lake

Buzzard
Roost Lake

Legend

▨ Area of Wetland Sites			
━━ Roads		𝕏 Hiking	
━━ Rivers		Δ Camping	
---- Hiking Trails		⊼ Picnic	
---- Boat Trails		♿ Handicap Access	
▥ Lakes		🏠 Cabins	
🛶 Canoeing		🚤 Boat Launch	
❀ Nature Study		✦ Fishing	
📷 Photography		⚹ Birdwatching	
♦ Visitor Center			

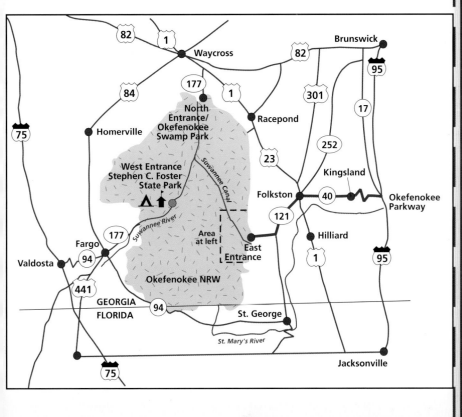

ecosystem. During times of drought, the swamp dries out, and lightning strikes during electrical storms cause the peat to smolder and burn. It does not take long for water levels in the swamp to drop when they are not being replenished by rainfall. On a hot summer day, evapotranspiration can reduce the water level in the Okefenokee by half an inch. Peat makes an excellent fuel and is even mined for that purpose elsewhere. In the Okefenokee, small, localized burns are a frequent occurrence. A massive, systemwide fire that burns deep into the peat occurs on a 20- to 30-year cycle.

Fire, it is said, keeps the swamp young. Fire is necessary to keep the swamp from filling in with vegetation and becoming a forest. Of course, the right fire at the wrong time, if it extends beyond refuge boundaries, can be devastating. According to local legend, one fire that was started when a kicking mule overturned a bucket of charcoal embers burned for 11 months in 1954-55. Known as the Mule Trail Fire, it burned 80 percent of the swamp and damaged thousands of acres of commercial timber outside the refuge. In 1990, a lightning strike ignited a fire that charred almost 21,000 acres and burned for three months. Prescribed burns are conducted periodically on the refuge to control the accumulation of excessive fuels and to promote the health of fire-dependent communities along the perimeter, such as the longleaf pine ecosystem. Because of the risk to adjacent, valuable timberlands, prescribed fire cannot be used within the swamp during the driest times when it would do the most good; consequently some of the Okefenokee's open prairie is being taken over by shrubs.

Fed by rainwater, which averages around 54 inches annually, the Okefenokee Swamp is not a completely closed basin. Actually, it drains slowly in a southwesterly direction. It is not strictly a swamp, but rather a slow-moving river of water overlying a peat bog contained in a shallow sand basin. The swamp serves as the headwaters for two key Southern rivers, the Suwannee and the St. Mary's. The Suwannee exits from the southwest corner of the swamp and eventually drains into the Gulf of Mexico. The St. Mary's rises from a gap in Trail Ridge on the refuge's eastern flank, serving to delineate the Georgia-Florida state line as the river meanders toward the Atlantic Ocean. There's even a River Styx in the extreme southeast corner of the Okefenokee, a name that serves as evidence of humankind's superstitious belief that swamps are dark, hellish places.

At one time, the Okefenokee was a land literally stalked by giants—not the proverbial giants of myths and legends but ancient, virgin cypress

Previous page: Cypress silhouettes along the Suwannee Canal
John Netherton

trees whose massive, towering trunks gave the swamp an air of grandeur and mystery. Unfortunately, this nation's historical disregard for wetlands reached a crescendo with efforts to ditch, drain, and log the Okefenokee. It commenced in 1890 with the founding of the Suwannee Canal Company, which purchased 258,000 acres of the Okefenokee from the state of Georgia for the fire-sale price of 26 cents an acre. The Atlanta-based firm intended to drain the swamp, cut and sell its timber, and then farm the land for cotton, corn, and rice. To that end, a drainage canal was dug eastward from the heart of the swamp, but it fell short of the intended endpoint, because the project was aborted due to prohibitive costs and the unforeseen enormity of the undertaking. Today, the 11.5-mile main canal serves as a waterway within the swamp for canoes and motorboats. If you take a guided trip from the concessionaire at the east entrance, it is the Suwannee Canal along which you will travel.

Before it folded, the Suwannee Canal Company took 11 million board feet of virgin cypress from the swamp. But that is just a knot on a log compared to what was cut and hauled away by the Hebard Cypress Company. This firm purchased 296,000 acres of the Okefenokee and took a staggering 420 million board feet of timber, mostly virgin cypress, between 1908 and 1927. Various other companies also logged the swamp at the same time. In order to haul the timber out of the swamp, 20-foot pilings were sunk through the peat and into the sandy floor below it, and 35 miles of railroad track penetrated the swamp's interior. Because freshly cut cypress trunks do not float, the trees were first "ringed," that is, the bark and sapwood were pierced, causing the tree to die so that it would dry and cure while still standing. It could then be felled and floated to waiting flatbed railcars.

At the height of the Hebard Company's logging operations, a town known as Hebardville (near Waycross) supported a population of a thousand workers. They so thoroughly logged the swamp that only two small stands of virgin cypress remained. For this reason, the Okefenokee has a more open and expansive look to it than one might imagine. The cypress that stand in the swamp today are rarely more than a hundred years old. You could say that the Okefenokee is currently in a period of ecological recovery that might be complete in a thousand years or so.

The Okefenokee was acquired in 1936 and established as a National Wildlife Refuge at the urging of conservation groups and, ironically, members of the Hebard family. Although the big trees have disappeared, so have signs of human activity and habitation. Today the refuge is a serene haven for wildlife. It can even be claimed that the successful comeback of the formerly endangered American alligator can be attributed to the Okefenokee. These great reptiles managed to maintain a breeding population within the boundaries of the Okefenokee National Wildlife Refuge during a time when they were being hunted and poached to near-extinction everywhere else for handbags and belts. The eventual passage of the Endangered Species Act made it illegal to trade in alligator hides, allowing the recovery of the species.

Presently, an estimated 10,000 alligators inhabit the Okefenokee. They can be seen floating in canals and lakes and basking on the banks throughout the swamp. They contribute to the health of the swamp and certain of its inhabitants by hollowing out "gator holes" (depressions) that, during periods of extended drought, contain some of the only standing water to be found in swamps like the Okefenokee.

One of the few species that preys upon the alligator is the Southern black bear, which finds gator nests and devours the eggs. The Southern black bear may soon be put on the federal Endangered Species List because its numbers have dropped to alarming levels due to poaching and habitat loss. As civilization increasingly presses upon plant and animal populations, the Okefenokee becomes ever more important as a reserve for species under assault.

Other rare or endangered species found here include the indigo snake, the red-cockaded woodpecker, and the gopher tortoise. Rumored sightings of the Florida panther, whose numbers are tragically low, remain unconfirmed. Other intriguing inhabitants include the bobcat and the red fox. The inventory of fauna on the refuge includes 64 reptile species, 50 mammals, 39 fish, and 37 amphibians, of which 21 are toads and frogs. The latter fill the swamp with their croaking, from the chirping of chorus frogs to the deep harumphing of bullfrogs. They are especially active on summer evenings.

Among the more distinctive features of the Okefenokee Swamp are its prairies: great, open expanses of flooded marsh covered with grasses, lily pads, and swamp iris. There are 60,000 acres of prairie within the Okefenokee, concentrated mainly in the east, with the most extensive being Grand and Chesser Prairies. They make ideal spots for birdwatching. A prime location at prairie's edge is the six-story Owl's Roost Tower at the end of the three-quarter mile "Swamp Walk," a wooden boardwalk that leads through dense cypress swamp into open prairie. Bird species counted at Okefenokee number 235, including winter visitors like the migratory greater sandhill crane and year-round residents like the Florida sandhill crane. These gray-colored natives, which reach five feet in height, let out a distinctive, hair-raising cry when alarmed. For this they have been dubbed "the watchmen of the swamp."

Owls Roost Tower overlooks Chesser Prairie and Seagrove Lake, offering a bird's-eye view of egrets, herons, cranes, and other wildlife ambling

Spanish moss-laden tree
John Netherton

around the prairie. From this treetop-level perch, visitors can survey a wetlands wilderness pulsing and teeming with life. While climbing the tower, notice how your footfalls cause the land to tremble. Allow plenty of time to stop, look, and listen to the goings-on in this intoxicating place.

Trails abound on the refuge. A system of wilderness canoe trails allows paddlers to get well out of range of civilization. Six blazed canoe trails criss-cross the swamp, making it possible to paddle across the Okefenokee from east to west (or vice versa) and from lake to lake. Four raised wooden platforms (measuring 20 feet by 28 feet) have been erected at intervals along the canoe trails for overnight camping, and stops are located on land. March and April are prime times for wilderness canoeing and camping in the Okefenokee, with trips limited to two nights due to popularity. Summer months expose canoeists to heat, humidity, mosquitoes, and deer flies; moreover, thunderstorms bring the danger of lightning, the single greatest hazard in the Okefenokee. Of course, that assumes you already know better than to disturb a hungry alligator.

Back on dry land, the refuge can be toured by car via Swamp Island Drive Trail, a 4.5-mile wildlife drive. You can stop along the drive to hike Upland Discovery Trail and a three-quarter mile boardwalk heading to an observation tower. Before setting out, drop by the visitor center to pick up annotated trail guides. Also be sure to visit the Chesser Island Homestead (stop No. 9 on the Swamp Island Drive Trail), where the grounds and buildings preserve a pioneer family's way of life on the edge of the swamp. Volunteers who greet the public at this site include folks who have spent their entire lives in the area and are walking encyclopedias of swamp life knowledge and lore.

The Okefenokee Swamp is a wonderful and unusual place—so much so that it enjoys international status and significance as a wetland. In 1971, an international convention held in Ramsar, Iran, adopted an accord that addressed the protection and preservation of wetlands. It is the only international agreement of an environmental nature that is devoted to a particular ecosystem type, and 92 nations have joined in adopting its objective of conserving wetlands. As part of the accord, 772 sites worldwide have been identified as "Wetlands of International Importance." These chosen wetlands must possess "international significance in terms of ecology, botany, zoology, limnology, or hydrology." The Okefenokee Swamp is the only Ramsar site in the 5-state Southeast region covered by this publication, and only 1 of 15 Ramsar sites in the entire United States.

A final word. There is now a proposal afoot to mine the entire Trail Ridge along the eastern boundary of the refuge. What impacts this may have on the Okefenokee is a matter that is currently under study. The point is that threats to this great swamp continue—as must our vigilance to protect it.

LOCATION There are three entrances to the Okefenokee Swamp. The main entrance is into the Okefenokee National Wildlife Refuge, on the east side. From Folkston, proceed south on GA 121 for 8 miles. Turn right at the entrance road into the refuge and follow to the visitor center. At the north end, Okefenokee Swamp Park lies 8 miles south of Waycross via U.S. 1. On the west side, Stephen C. Foster State Park is located 17 miles east of Fargo along GA 177.

WHEN IT'S OPEN Entrance hours at Okefenokee Wildlife Refuge vary seasonally; check with the office for current schedule. The visitor center is open 10:00 a.m. to 4:00 p.m. daily. The Suwannee Canal Recreation Concession, which leads guided boat tours, rents equipment, and takes reservations for overnight canoe trails, is open 7:00 a.m. to 7:30 p.m. (March 1 through September 10) and 8:00 a.m. to 6:00 p.m. (September 11 through February 28). At Stephen C. Foster State Park, park gate hours are 7:00 a.m. to 7:00 p.m. (September 15 through March 1) and 6:30 a.m. to 8:30 p.m. (March 2 through September 14). Office hours are 8:00 a.m. to 5:00 p.m. daily. Okefenokee Swamp Park is open 9:00 a.m. to 6:30 p.m. in summer and 9:00 a.m. to 5:30 p.m. the rest of the year.

BEST TIMES TO VISIT Fall bird migration begins in September with the arrival of warblers, and cooler weather brings better fishing, too. Wildflowers begin blooming in March. Birdwatching is good all year, but is especially so from January through April. The summer months pose hazards and inconveniences that canoeists should be aware of, including the ever-present threat of electrical storms and the presence of biting insects.

WHAT TO DO Birdwatching, guided boat trips, canoeing, camping, fishing, walking, photography, and nature study.

WHERE TO STAY Camping is permitted on raised platforms along wilderness canoe trails in Okefenokee National Wildlife Refuge. Reservations are necessary and can be made as far as two months in advance of the date of arrival. For reservations, contact the Okefenokee National Wildlife Refuge (912-496-3331) between 7:00 a.m. and 10:00 a.m. There are ground-level campsites for tents and RVs and cottages for overnight rental at Stephen C. Foster State Park. Motels and camping areas are available in Folkston and Waycross.

FOR MORE INFORMATION Okefenokee National Wildlife Refuge, Route 2, Box 3330, Folkston, GA 31537 (912-496-7836); Stephen C. Foster State Park, Route 1, Box 131, Fargo, GA 31631 (912-637-5274); Okefenokee Swamp Park, 5700 Okefenokee Swamp Park Road, Waycross, GA 31501 (912-283-0583).

GEORGIA

Skidaway Island

WETLANDS TYPES:

High and low salt marsh

Royal terns with chicks
Tom Blagden, Jr.

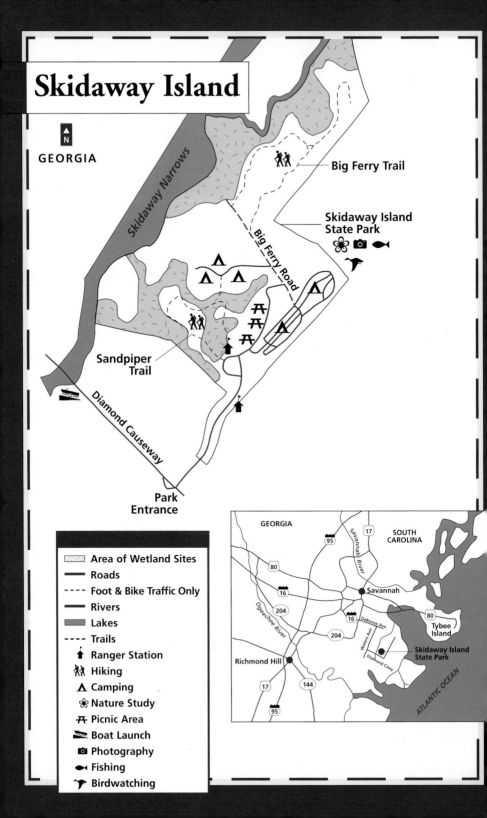

Skidaway Island

GEORGIA

Big Ferry Trail

Skidaway Island State Park

Big Ferry Road

Skidaway Narrows

Sandpiper Trail

Diamond Causeway

Park Entrance

Legend

- Area of Wetland Sites
- Roads
- Foot & Bike Traffic Only
- Rivers
- Lakes
- Trails
- Ranger Station
- Hiking
- Camping
- Nature Study
- Picnic Area
- Boat Launch
- Photography
- Fishing
- Birdwatching

GEORGIA

SOUTH CAROLINA

Savannah River

95

17

80

16

204

Ogeechee River

16

DeRenne Ave.

Savannah

80

Tybee Island

204

Waters Ave.

Skidaway Island State Park

Richmond Hill

17

144

Diamond Cwy.

95

ATLANTIC OCEAN

I t was not easy choosing just one salt marsh on the Georgia coast to write about. The area between Georgia's barrier islands and the mainland, a belt that is between four to eight miles wide, is seemingly one unending salt marsh. If the Midwest can be celebrated for its "amber waves of grain," the Georgia coast surely merits acclaim for its "golden isles of grass," for they are remarkable in their own right. Actually, poet and native son Sidney Lanier canonized the Georgia coast for all time with his reverential poem "The Marshes of Glynn," written about the salt marshes in and around Brunswick that so enthralled him while he was growing up.

It is easy to share his enthusiasm for salt marshes. They are among the most productive environments in the world (as measured by annual yield in grams of organic carbon per square meter) and are necessary to the health of coastal fisheries. Moreover, they are appealing to look at. Water flows in and out with the tides, inundating the low marsh for part of the day and then leaving exposed expanses of salt-marsh grasses bathed in golden sunlight and swaying with the breeze.

Marsh crabs and mud fiddlers scuttle about, while delicate white periwinkle snails move up and down cordgrass stalks as water levels rise and recede. Ribbed mussels attach themselves to the stalk bases with byssal threads. All the while, cordgrass goes indomitably about its business in an inhospitable environment. When it dies, the dead cordgrass—known as "wrack"—becomes a critical part of the food chain both in the salt marsh and the open ocean into which it is carried by ebbing tides. Driven by cordgrass, you can sense a giant photosynthetic engine churning quietly out on the salt marsh.

The salt marshes along the Georgia coast are sufficiently uniform that to write about one is to write about all. The state's relatively compact coastline, which runs for about a hundred miles from Tybee Island (near Savannah) to Cumberland Island (by the Florida state line), lies at the head of the South Atlantic Bight—a fact that is largely responsible for the considerable range of its tides and the extent of its salt marshes.

The South Atlantic Bight runs from Cape Hatteras, North Carolina, to Miami, Florida. At each end, the tidal exchange is from one to three feet. But at the center of the bight—around Jekyll and St. Simons Islands, at the head of the Georgia embayment—water piles up as it funnels into the inward-curving coastline. As a result, the tidal exchange along the Georgia coast is much greater, averaging six to nine feet. The marked difference between tides that ebb and flow across the gradually sloping Coastal Plain means that a tremendous area on the Georgia coast is flooded at high tide and exposed at low tide. This has allowed an extensive and intricate network of marshes to develop. Although its coastline is short, Georgia lays claim to a half million acres of salt marsh—nearly a third of all the salt marsh area on the East Coast.

If you want to study salt marshes, Georgia is the place to come. Along its coast are eight barrier-island clusters: Tybee and Little Tybee Islands; Skidaway and Wassaw Islands; Ossabaw Island; St. Catherines Island; Blackbeard, Sapelo, and Wolf Islands; Little St. Simons, St. Simons, and Sea Islands; Jekyll Island; and Little Cumberland and Cumberland Islands. The younger, outermost islands are of Holocene origin, having formed approximately 18,000 years ago as the last Ice Age receded and sea levels rose, pushing the sand sheet up the continental slope. Adjoining, overlapping, and paralleling these Holocene-era barrier islands is a chain of islands that includes Skidaway. These are considerably older, having formed 35,000 to 40,000 years ago during the Pleistocene epoch. They lie behind, and are sometimes welded to, the Holocene islands. Extending as far inland as the eastern rim of the Okefenokee Swamp, five more sand ridges on the mainland have been identified as ancient barrier island profiles.

The well-formed salt marshes along the Georgia coast are dominated by a single plant—*Spartina alterniflora,* or "smooth cordgrass," which is ingeniously adapted to surviving in areas of high salinity. Another salt-tolerant *Spartina* species, *S. patens,* is a shorter, more fine-leafed relative that flourishes in the salt marshes north of North Carolina's Pamlico Sound. It is less common in the Deep South. *Spartina*'s task is neither an easy nor an enviable one. Not only does it tolerate salinity, but it also must cope with twice-daily periods of inundation and desiccation. It is truly one of the wonders of nature. To describe the way it works is beyond the scope of this essay. Briefly, *Spartina* manages to raise its internal concentration of salts to a level where an osmotic pressure gradient allows the plant to effectively draw in freshwater from seawater. Of this coarse-leafed colonizer of salt marshes, which can reach heights of six feet or more, writers/scientists John and Mildred Teal had this to say in their classic study, *Life and Death of the Salt Marsh:*

> "*Spartina* survives in the hostile atmosphere of the salt marsh and endures the sea by keeping most of the salt out of its sap, by secreting what little salt does get into the sap, and by concentrating some of this same salt in its cells so that they will be able to resist the tension placed upon the sap by the evaporation occurring through the stomata. It is a success story of the most complicated nature. The entire system has been constructed by natural selection so that it functions with great economy."

Great egret in a salt marsh near the edge of a maritime forest, by John Netherton

While cordgrass is dominant along the marshes of the Georgia coast, other plants also can be found if you look closely. These include spikegrass (*Distichlis spicata*) and glassworts (*Salicornia* sp.). *Distichlis* is a short grass with a distinctively spiky arrangement of blades. *Salicornia* is a succulent marsh dweller—also known as pickleplant or pickleweed—that is sometimes used in salads. These plants are found on the less regularly flooded high marsh.

Zonation across a salt marsh yields plant communities that vary according to differential exposure to salt, water, and temperature. Tidal creeks meander through the marsh, filling and draining it twice daily. At peak inflow, the creek beds overflow their banks, inundating the marsh flats. Mud-bank levees higher than the surrounding marsh border the creeks. It is

here that the tallest strands of cordgrass are found. Beyond the levees are the low marsh (claimed almost exclusively by cordgrass) and high marsh (a sandier, saltier area typically covered with water for an hour or less each day). The high marsh features *Spartina alterniflora* in stunted form, *S. patens*, and salt-tolerant plants like glasswort and spikegrass. Salt concentrations in certain areas on the high marsh reach extremes that no plant can tolerate. These areas, known as salt pans, appear barren of life and are recognizable by a crystalline whiteness at the surface.

Above the high marsh is the marsh border. It is an area of reduced salinity where freshwater runoff from storms dilutes what marginal tidal influence is felt. Clumps of black needlegrass rush (*Juncus roemerianus*) appear along the upper border of the high marsh, although it is a more pronounced feature of freshwater marshes and river margins at the upper ends of estuaries. From here, the marsh border yields to transitional communities whose upper elevational reaches are occupied by forested islands known as hammocks.

All of these environments can be viewed at Skidaway Island, an ancient barrier island southeast of Savannah (and due west of Wassaw Island). Occupying the northwest corner of the island, bordering the Intracoastal Waterway, is Skidaway Island State Park. This 533-acre park runs the gamut from salt marsh to oak, pine, and palm-covered hammocks. Two park trails explore the island's varied environments. The mile-long Sandpiper Trail is a partially boardwalked path over and through the high marsh, skirting the edge of tidal creeks and passing by barren salt pans. Big Ferry Trail is a two-mile loop that can be extended to a three-mile hike if you take a spur trail out to some historic gun sills and emplacements. In terms of natural features, Big Ferry Trail runs along the Intracoastal Waterway and through woodlands that include live oak, longleaf pine, cabbage palmetto, redbay, magnolia, and American holly. A three-deck, 30-foot observation tower in a hammock overlooks the Intracoastal Waterway, making a great birdwatching perch.

With its salt marsh, tidal estuaries, and maritime forest, Skidaway is typical of Georgia's barrier island chain. What is unusual about it is its accessibility. Park facilities include a campground and picnic shelters. Four miles away is Skidaway Marine Institute, an oceanographic research center that is part of Georgia's state university system. The institute's aquarium is open to the public for a modest charge and is well worth visiting.

Previous page: Sunset over oyster beds
Tom Blagden, Jr.

If this taste of a Georgia salt marsh makes you hungry for more, consider visiting one or both of the Georgia sea islands that are accessible to the public. Trips to Sapelo Island, a barrier island near Darien, are conducted by the Georgia Department of Natural Resources. The National Park Service runs passenger ferries to Cumberland Island off the southern Georgia coast near the Florida line. Both afford unmatched opportunities to explore the barrier-island environment—wide, sandy beaches, maritime forests, and extensive salt marshes—in all its undisturbed glory.

LOCATION Skidaway Island is located southeast of Savannah. From downtown, head south on Waters Avenue for six miles to Montgomery Crossroads and continue on Whitefield Avenue, which merges with Diamond Causeway and leads over the Intracoastal Waterway onto Skidaway Island. Follow signs to Skidaway Island State Park. To get to the Skidaway Marine Institute Aquarium, continue east on Diamond Causeway past the state park entrance and turn left on McWhorter Road. Follow to the north end of the island. The aquarium is on the left and is identified by a ship's wheel and anchor.

WHEN IT'S OPEN Skidaway Island State Park is open 7:00 a.m. to 10:00 p.m. Park office hours are 8:00 a.m. to 5:00 p.m. Skidaway Marine Institute Aquarium is open 9:00 a.m. to 4:00 p.m., Monday through Friday, and noon to 5:00 p.m. on Saturday.

BEST TIMES TO VISIT Fall is especially pleasant on Skidaway Island; the cooler weather cuts down on the bugs.

WHAT TO DO Camping, hiking, birdwatching, picnicking, fishing, photography, and nature study.

WHERE TO STAY Skidaway Island State Park has an 88-site campground for tents and RVs. Hotels, motels, and inns are abundant in nearby Savannah.

FOR MORE INFORMATION Skidaway Island State Park, 52 Diamond Causeway, Savannah, GA 31411 (912-598-2300). For information on the barrier islands mentioned at the end of the text, contact Sapelo Island National Estuarine Reserve (912-485-2299) and Cumberland Island National Seashore (912-882-4336).

Badin Upland Depression Swamps

WETLANDS TYPES:

Upland depression swamp forest

Woodlands in Uwharrie National Forest
John Netherton

O ne of the most interesting wetland sites in this survey will not be identified on any map. There are no trails that lead to Badin Upland Depression Swamps, located in North Carolina's Uwharrie National Forest, near the town of Troy in the center of the state. To get there, you should have in hand a 7.5-minute United States Geological Survey topographic map of the Badin Quadrangle (available at Uwharrie National Forest headquarters), a compass, and, ideally, some prior orientation from Forest Service personnel. The Badin Upland Depression Swamps are reachable by driving on gravel Forest Service roads to a point on Forest Road 576 roughly a quarter of a mile west of its junction with Forest Road 516. From here, hike up an unnamed mountain in an easterly direction for a half mile. The swamps are located inside the 700-foot-elevation contour on the USGS topographic map, about a half mile east of the Badin Dam.

With any luck, you should wind up at or near a pair of adjacent waterlogged depressions, shaped like elongated ovals, that occupy two and three acres apiece. These are the Badin Upland Depression Swamps. They are, perhaps, the last thing you would expect to find at the top of a hill. The larger one is oriented on a north-south axis and lies just north of the smaller one, which runs east-west. It has been theorized that solution of the underlying mafic volcanic rock may be the cause of these wet depressions. In any case, they contrast sharply with the dry forest surrounding them. The water level varies seasonally, with the swamps remaining wet most of the year but drying up during the summer months. The water is deepest and the depressions are most extensive in the late winter and early spring. At this time, several species of amphibians—including large populations of marbled (*Ambystoma opacum*) and spotted (*A. maculatum*) salamanders—come from miles around to breed, leaving sticky egg masses in the water.

This wetland type and its associated community is limited to Virginia and the Carolinas, and it is rare even in this region. Therefore, the Badin Upland Depression Swamps have been registered as a Natural Heritage Area by the state of North Carolina and as a Special Interest Natural Area by the U.S. Forest Service. The swamps are indeed an unusual and magical place. During a late fall visit, they were inundated to a depth of several inches, and the glistening shallows stood in marked contrast to the surrounding hillsides, which were covered with dry, dead leaves.

The trees that inhabit the depressions are also different, tending toward water-tolerant bottomland hardwood species rather than the dry oak-hickory forest around them. Overcup oak, willow oak, and blackgum—

Sphagnum moss and mushroom, by John Netherton

all typical of Coastal Plains bottomlands—are found in the canopy. Trees in
the subcanopy include swamp chestnut oak and green ash. Wetlands shrubs,
such as buttonbush and arrowwood, which are more commonly found in
Coastal Plains swamps, grow in the depressions. The herbaceous layer is
composed of sedges, rushes, thorny vines, the Atamasco lily, and various
mosses. By contrast, the surrounding forest is a mixed stand of hickories,
less water-tolerant oaks, and occasional cedars, with the subcanopy consist-
ing of dogwood, red maple, and sourwood. There are virtually no shrubs
or herbaceous layers away from the depressions, which gives the woods an
open look and makes for easy walking. Boulders and rock outcroppings,
however, are common.

The Badin Upland Depression Swamps represent an esoteric,
though fascinating, niche in the wetlands typology. Herpetologists and
wetlands scientists are the likeliest to seek them out, although the hunting
blind that stands at the edge of the north depression is evidence that scientists

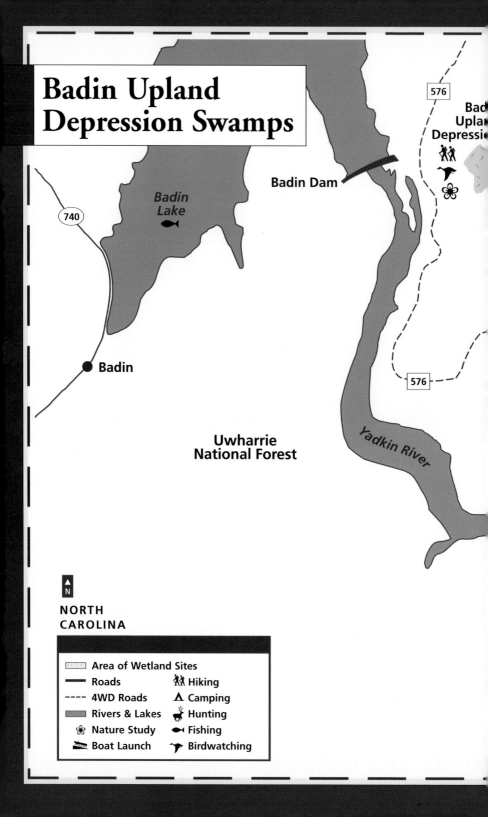

Badin Upland Depression Swamps

Badin Dam

Badin Lake

740

576

Bad
Upla
Depressi

Badin

Uwharrie
National Forest

Yadkin River

576

N

NORTH
CAROLINA

Area of Wetland Sites
Roads
4WD Roads
Rivers & Lakes
Nature Study
Boat Launch

Hiking
Camping
Hunting
Fishing
Birdwatching

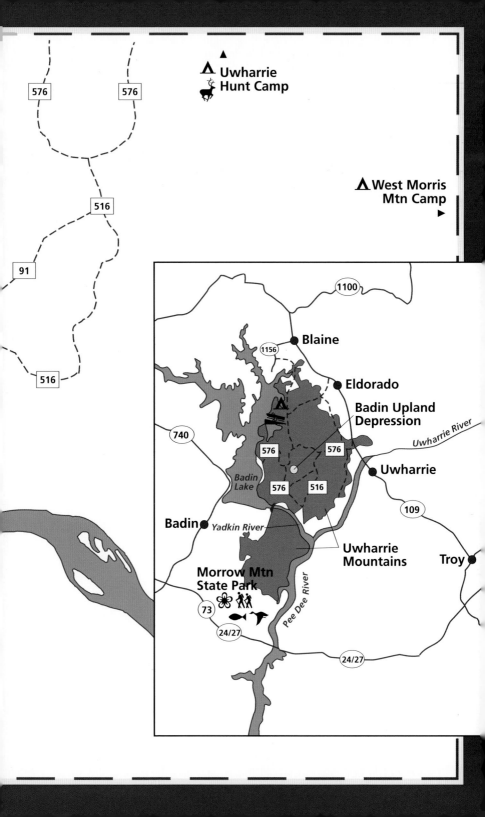

are not the only visitors. Given their limited extent and biological unique-ness, they should be treated as a precious component of the unique natural heritage of the region. If you come, be a cautious, respectful observer.

The swamps occur within the Uwharrie National Forest, which itself offers much in the way of outdoor recreation. The low Uwharries, with elevations around 1,000 feet, are possibly the oldest mountains on the North American continent. Formed by volcanic and metamorphic activity when the African and North American plates collided 500 million years ago, scientists believe the Uwharries once rose to heights of 20,000 feet. Erosion over the unfathomable millennia has reduced them to the rounded, rolling hills of the present day. Archaeological finds include spear points and stone scraping tools that have been dated to 12,000 B.C. A sophisticated culture of Creek Indians farmed and thrived here from 1,000 B.C. until the arrival of European settlers in the 1700s.

The nation's first gold rush occurred not in California but in the Uwharries, where gold was struck in 1799. The area gave rise to 274 mines in 14 counties, and gold mining continued until the Great Depression. Even today, flakes of gold are still found here. Would-be prospectors pan for gold dust in the streams, and permits to explore for gold, copper, and zinc are occasionally filed. More commonly, though, people come to camp, hike, fish, and watch for bald eagles. These grand raptors are frequently spotted at the base of Badin Dam, where they find a ready source of food in fish that have been mangled in their inadvertent passage through the dam's turbines.

LOCATION To get to the Badin Upland Depression Swamps from the town of Troy, take NC 109 north for ten miles, turn left at the sign for Badin Lake and follow for 0.4 mile to Forest Road 576. Turn right and follow for five miles. Park by the side of road and walk in an easterly direction up the hillside for 0.5 mile. Consult personnel at the District Ranger's Office for Uwharrie National Forest, the USGS topographic map for the Badin Quadrangle, and the above text for more explicit directions. The Uwharrie National Forest District Office is located two miles east of Troy on NC 27.

WHEN IT'S OPEN Uwharrie National Forest is open year round for camp-ing and hiking. The District Ranger's Office is open 8:00 a.m. to 4:30 p.m., Monday through Friday.

BEST TIMES TO VISIT The depressions are under water from early spring to the end of May. Bald eagles can most often be seen in the vicinity of Badin Dam from December through February. Fall is an excellent time to see the changing colors in the Uwharries.

WHAT TO DO Hiking, camping (developed and primitive sites), hunting, fishing, birdwatching, picnicking, and nature study. Morrow Mountain State Park is located on the west side of Yadkin River and offers much to do in the outdoors as well.

WHERE TO STAY There is a developed campground at Badin Lake (37 sites), with water, toilets, tables, and grills. A more recently developed facility, Arrowhead Campground (also at Badin Lake), has 54 sites, 15 with electrical hookups. A large bath house has showers, toilets, and baby-changing stations. Some sites are large enough for RVs. A half-mile trail surrounds this facility, and there are picnic tables and grills. Uwharrie Hunt Camp (8 sites) and West Morris Mountain (14 sites) are for tent camping only. Backpackers can camp anywhere on national forest land except at designated wildlife fields and trailhead parking lots.

FOR MORE INFORMATION Uwharrie National Forest, District Ranger's Office, Route 3, Box 470, Troy, NC 27371 (910-576-6391).

Green Swamp Preserve

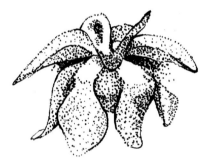

WETLANDS TYPES:

Low pocosin and wet longleaf pine savanna

Trumpet-leaf pitcher-plant
John Netherton

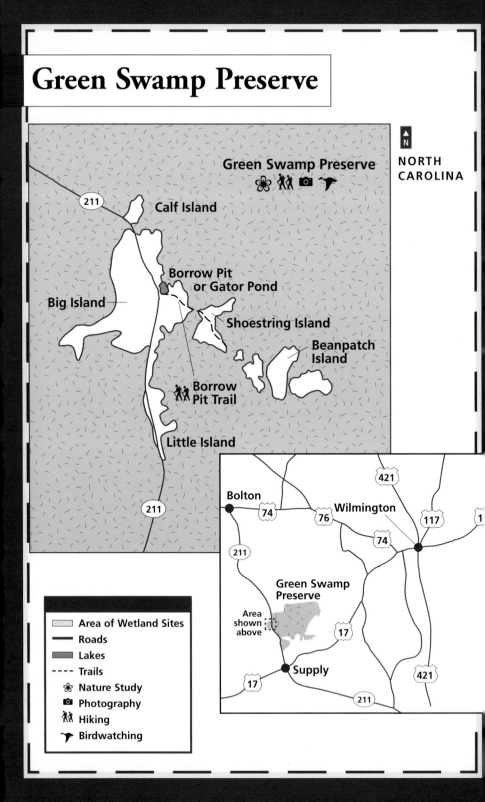

Green Swamp Preserve

Green Swamp Preserve

NORTH CAROLINA

211

Calf Island

Borrow Pit
or Gator Pond

Big Island

Shoestring Island

Beanpatch
Island

Borrow
Pit Trail

Little Island

211

421

Bolton

74

Wilmington

76

117

1

211

74

Green Swamp
Preserve

17

Area
shown
above

17

421

17

Supply

211

Area of Wetland Sites
Roads
Lakes
Trails
Nature Study
Photography
Hiking
Birdwatching

G reen Swamp Preserve is a fine example of two associated wetland types: pocosins (which are relatively tangled and inhospitable but fascinating) and savannas (which are open, meadowlike, and beautiful). The area of overlap between them is the favored habitat of rare and unique insectivorous species such as the Venus flytrap, pitcher-plant, and sundew.

Pocosins are forbidding places. No wetland is more impenetrable. They are highly unusual in their hydrology and faunal makeup, being geographically limited to the Southeast—especially North Carolina, where 70 percent of all remaining pocosins are found. Pocosins constitute a maze of scrubby, low-lying vegetation and stunted pines found in organic-rich but nutrient-poor soils. They typically occur on poorly drained interstream divides on the Coastal Plain, having formed during a period of sea level rise 8,000 to 10,000 years ago. It is theorized that the rising ocean created the conditions for pocosin formation by causing backed-up rivers to deposit sediment loads across the Coastal Plain, resulting in blocked drainage and peat accumulation.

In a sense, the ruggedness of pocosins has helped ensure their survival, since these spongy, waterlogged peatlands are tough to develop. However, pocosins and associated wetlands have been catastrophically impacted, with vast areas drained and cleared for farming and forestry. As recently as 1950, pocosins accounted for 16 percent (908,000 acres) of the total land area for North Carolina's 41 coastal counties. Only 31 percent of the pocosins that existed at mid-decade remained unaltered by 1980. For example, all that survives of the once-massive Green Swamp, which formerly occupied more than 170,000 acres of cypress-gum and white cedar swamp forest and pocosin on the Coastal Plain, is a 15,722-acre preserve deeded to The Nature Conservancy.

The surviving pocket of pocosin known as Green Swamp Preserve is too dense and inaccessible to make commercial exploitation economically feasible. It perseveres almost as an act of defiance. Its spongy, scrubby interior contains a suite of species that include pond pine, various bays (sweetbay, redbay, and loblolly bay), gallberry holly, greenbrier, and such common low-pocosin shrubs as titi, fetterbush, and zenobia. Mammals that find refuge on the pocosin include deer, black bear, bobcat, and gray squirrel. Reptile inhabitants include the eastern diamondback rattlesnake and American alligator, both classified as state endangered species. A wooden walkway on the Green Swamp Preserve briefly crosses the pocosin, affording an up-close glimpse into its dense, low-lying thickets.

Pocosins are broadly divided into two classes: scrub-shrub pocosin (a.k.a. low pocosin), which is dominated by a vegetative cover less than six feet in height; and forested pocosin (a.k.a. high pocosin), whose dominant plant species exceed six feet in height. Low pocosin is found on large, deep deposits of peat, while high pocosin lies atop a thinner peat layer underlain by mineral soils. Pocosins are ecologically related to Carolina bays and bay forests in that they harbor similar flora and fauna. All pocosins are palustrine wetlands that are primarily oligotrophic—that is, they receive nutrient input solely from rainwater—and lack natural drainage outlets.

Pocosins sometimes occur in association with savannas, which are grassy flatlands with a scattering of longleaf pines. The savanna "islands" in Green Swamp are mostly high areas along an ancient shoreline escarpment. However, some of the smaller islands appear to be the sand rims of Carolina bays that have been swallowed up by the accumulating peat deposits. The soils in a savanna are more mineralized and therefore support a richly diverse association of plants. Even more diverse are the ecotones— areas of overlap—between savanna and pocosin. As many as 50 plant species per square meter have been cataloged here. It is these overlapping margins that harbor the heaviest concentration of rare, insectivorous species unique to the region. These, as well as all other areas of the savannas, are extremely sensitive to foot traffic.

The Nature Conservancy's Green Swamp Preserve offers an opportunity, right off the highway, to explore a pocosin-savanna complex. An unmarked trail begins at a pullout on Highway 211, leading through an old "pine plantation"—an area managed for timber production—to a pristine savanna known as Shoestring Island. Here in the midst of the pocosin's thorny tangle lies an open oasis that supports an impressive stand of longleaf pine and a vast understory of wiregrass.

The trailhead can be found at the head of the pullout area, which lies on the south side of Borrow Pit Pond. (Pottery shards dating back 2,000 years have been found near the pond.) Informally named Borrow Pit Trail, the trail is only open through Shoestring Island, approximately one mile. However, you do not need to hike that far to appreciate the varied make-up of this unusual landscape. The first half mile takes in a slash pine plantation, proceeds over a boardwalk through pond pine woodland, and enters the prairielike savanna of Shoestring Island. It is difficult to convey the tranquility one feels in the midst of this majestic Coastal Plain savanna, with its towering pines and verdant understory of wiregrass and wildflowers. It is home to rare animal species such as fox squirrel, mimic glass lizard, and Carolina

*Clockwise from upper left: Rosebud orchid,
grass pink, sweet pitcher-plant*
John Netherton

gopher frog, as well as the federally
protected red-cockaded woodpecker,
which is the keystone species of the
longleaf pine ecosystem.

These woodpeckers are dependent upon longleaf pines, and the
decline in habitat—due to the fact that longleafs grow too slowly to be of
economic benefit to the timber industry, taking 70 to 80 years to reach a
harvestable height—has reduced the woodpecker's numbers to critical levels.
Fortunately, habitat restoration, such as that undertaken at Green Swamp
Preserve, is promoting the bird's comeback. If you are lucky, you might
see a red-cockaded woodpecker noisily fussing about the mastlike heights
of a longleaf pine, where it has carved out a cavity in the tree's heartwood.
Despite such sightings, the fact remains that these woodpeckers are still
struggling for survival. According to Nature Conservancy biologists, the
local population remains tenuously stable. There are also concerns that

the small population will lead to inbreeding, which would further put the species at risk.

Another problem in the preserve is poaching. Apparently, some unscrupulous nurseries in the Wilmington area pay local poachers the equivalent of beer money to raid the Green Swamp of one of its treasures—the Venus flytrap. A hardy plant, it is nonetheless so limited in geographical extent that its removal from the Green Swamp amounts to pirating a valued element of North Carolina's natural heritage. Typically, poachers are dropped by the side of the road, disappearing into the woods to fill garbage bags with hastily unearthed flytraps. During the summer of 1995, The Nature Conservancy's Wilmington office received more than one call a day reporting poaching activities in the Green Swamp Preserve. The income received from the plundering of the Venus flytrap in no way compensates for the loss, and conscionable consumers should avoid purchasing them.

On a more upbeat note, the area is being successfully fire-managed by The Nature Conservancy, which oversees periodic burns mimicking lightning strikes that occurred naturally before settlement by Europeans and the landscape changes that resulted. Some of the plants in the area, particularly the native pines, actually rely on fire to trigger the release of seeds from their cones. When fire is suppressed in a fire-dependent community, a buildup of fuel on the floor creates a potential tinderbox that can burn out of control in a way that nature never intended. Therefore, periodic managed burns are conducted by The Nature Conservancy, with assistance from the U.S. Forest Service.

The results can be seen at Shoestring Island, which is covered with chest-high stands of wiregrass, with seed-bearing tops that are soft and feathery. Below this herbaceous canopy, beautiful purple and yellow wildflowers add splashes of color. Still closer to the ground grow the fascinating flytraps, their bristly, parted shells waiting to snare an unsuspecting insect—one ingenious adaptation to the problem of nutrient-poor soil. Other carnivorous flora are found along the pocosin-savanna ecotone as well. The small, ground-level sundew is recognized by its reddish, radiating leaves with hairs that secrete a sticky substance that attracts and traps insects. Then there are the four species of pitcher-plant: trumpet-leaf, sweet, purple, and hooded. Insects are first numbed by a substance secreted inside the plant's rim and then drowned in rainwater collected in its container. (***Note:*** These

Previous page: Green Swamp savanna with longleaf pines
John Netherton

and other plant species are very popular subjects for photographers. However, the act of getting on one's knees to position the camera can damage the area, and over time, degrade the habitat. The use of a telephoto lens is therefore recommended.) Another curiosity found here is known as toothache grass. Although it looks nondescript, rubbing it on one's gums induces a temporary numbing effect.

It is interesting to observe the differences between pine plantation and undisturbed savanna. The paper company's slash pines grow in ruler-straight rows along foot-high ridges dug by heavy machinery. In a system where even minute shifts in elevation produce observable changes in ecological makeup, these undulating, machine-made gradients pose a problem for habitat restoration at Green Swamp Preserve and wherever such land may eventually be reclaimed. At Shoestring Island, however, the longleaf pine-wiregrass ecosystem remains intact and undisturbed. As for the pocosin, you must pass through it to get to the pine savanna. And although no one will ever wax sentimental about pocosins, you have to admire their defiant hardiness.

LOCATION The path into Green Swamp Preserve is located seven miles north of Supply on the east side of Highway 211.

WHEN IT'S OPEN The Green Swamp Preserve is private property owned by The Nature Conservancy. Official Nature Conservancy field trips are offered as a benefit to members, and staff will lead a limited number of tours for other groups as time permits. Individuals who want to visit the preserve are asked to call The Nature Conservancy's Wilmington office (910-762-6277) for permission.

BEST TIMES TO VISIT All year, but especially in spring for wildflowers.

WHAT TO DO Hiking, birdwatching, and nature study.

WHERE TO STAY A wide range of accommodations is available in the city of Wilmington, 30 miles away.

FOR MORE INFORMATION The Nature Conservancy, 321 North Front Street, Wilmington, NC 28401 (910-762-6277).

Lake Mattamuskeet

WETLANDS TYPES:

Lacustrine and freshwater marshes

Forested shore of Lake Mattamuskeet
John Netherton

L ake Mattamuskeet is the largest lake in North Carolina and one of the few naturally occuring lakes of any size found in the Southeast. With just a few exceptions, all other lakes in the region were created by damming, either by beavers or humans. Popular theories have held that Lake Mattamuskeet was scoured by meteors or hollowed out by lightning-caused fires that burned deeply into the peat. Indian lore tells of a peat fire lasting "thirteen moons." *Mattamuskeet* is an Algonquin Indian word meaning "dry dust," which might allude to the aftereffects of the peat fire. Whatever the cause, this lake is part of a system of lakes, ponds, swamps, forests, pocosins, and meadows strung across the Coastal Plain of the Carolinas. Such a system is found nowhere else in the world.

Lake Mattamuskeet is the centerpiece of Mattamuskeet National Wildlife Refuge, located in Hyde County, on the Albemarle-Pamlico Peninsula. This part of the state is generally passed through by vacationers heading to the Outer Banks. Yet with three other national wildlife refuges—Swanquarter, Alligator River, and Pocosin Lakes—in close proximity to Mattamuskeet, it deserves to become a destination for those who love the outdoors. This network of refuges occupies 325,000 acres in east-central North Carolina, encompassing wooded swamps, scrubby pocosins, brackish and freshwater marshes, and mixed pine-hardwood forests.

The lake is 18 miles long and varies between 5 and 6 miles wide. It is quite shallow, with an average depth of 2.5 feet and a maximum depth of 5 feet at its western end. Because it is a wind- and wave-driven system—unlike, for instance, the still, static waters of Merchants Millpond (see separate entry)—the surface of Lake Mattamuskeet is clear and free of duckweed, water lilies, algal blooms, and other floating vegetation. Four canals dug in the late 1800s and early 1900s connect Lake Mattamuskeet with Pamlico Sound. A system of gated, wooden structures permits outflow when necessary and prevents the inflow of brackish water from the sound, which would alter the lake's ecology and biochemistry.

Although it is the largest natural lake in the Carolinas, it was at one time even larger by a third, occupying 60,000 acres instead of its present 40,000. The reduction in size resulted from attempts to drain the lake for agricultural purposes. Instead of clearing the pocosins and forests, which demanded considerable and difficult labor, it was believed that the lake bottom would make excellent farmland if it were ditched and drained. Canals were dug as far back as the early 1800s, but not until 1911 did these efforts seriously affect lake levels and acreage. Over the next 20 years, three different owners grappled with the great lake. Yet despite the best available

Tundra swans, by John Netherton

pumping technology—including what was then the world's largest pumping station, capable of pumping 1.25 million gallons per minute—the lake prevailed, and all who attempted to drain and farm it went bankrupt.

The most historically significant attempt at drainage and cultivation was made by August Hecksher, a wealthy New York philanthropist. Unlike the previous owners, Hecksher was able to cultivate 13,000 acres of lake bed in corn and soybeans. But even his high-tech ways were too costly to turn a profit, and his New Holland Corporation went bankrupt in 1932. Hecksher sold his 50,000-acre holdings to the U.S. Fish and Wildlife Service in 1934, and Mattamuskeet was established as a migratory bird refuge at that time.

Today, Lake Mattamuskeet serves as one of the most valuable wintering areas for migratory waterfowl along the Atlantic flyway. They begin arriving in October. By January of each year, the number of winged visitors totals over 150,000. These include 100,000 ducks, 35,000 tundra swans, 10,000 snow geese, and 5,000 Canada geese. Twenty species of ducks are seasonal visitors. Many seek out the 13 impoundments that have been

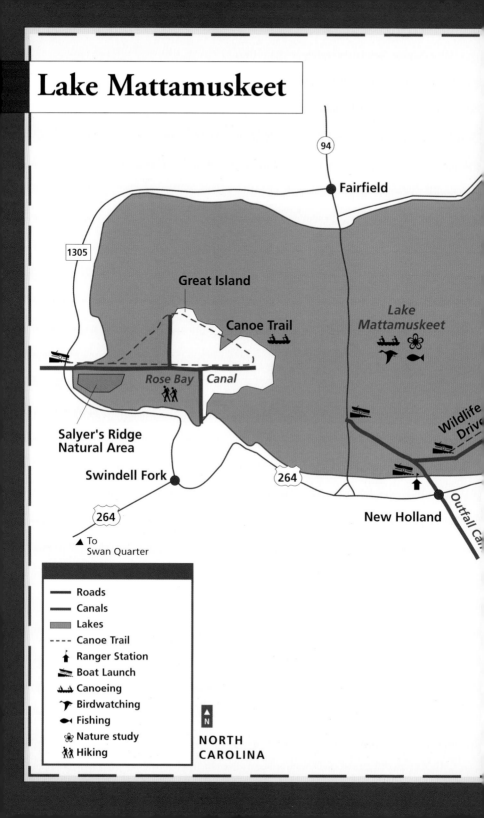

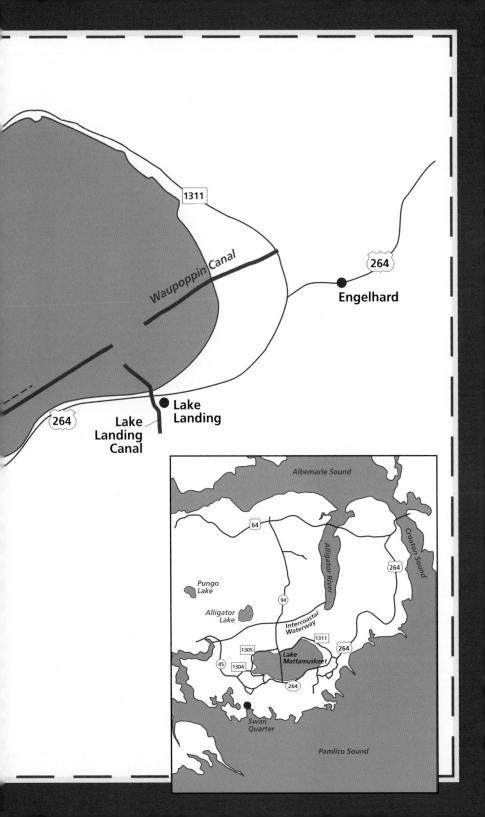

created on the refuge. Among the duck populations, dabblers generally prefer the impoundments while divers frequent deeper waters. Between the emergent vegetation of the shallows and the submerged aquatic vegetation along the lake bottom, the area provides a smorgasbord of food for over-wintering waterfowl. Favored aquatic vegetation includes wild celery and redhead grass, which are abundant on Lake Mattamuskeet. The impound-ments are managed so that they remain in an early successional stage of development. To do so means ridding them of unwanted species like common reed (*Phragmites* sp.), which move into areas where soils have been disturbed, as was the case in Lake Mattamuskeet's farming past.

One-half of the entire population of great, graceful tundra swans (a.k.a. whistling swans) makes its way to North Carolina from Alaska and northwestern Canada. Summer inhabitants include ospreys who build nests in stunted cypress trees, another unusual feature of the lake. These dwarf cypress, unlike their hundred-foot counterparts routinely found in swamps throughout the South, are no more than eight feet tall—bonsai cypress, as it were. A good vantage point for viewing everything from marshy impound-ments to dwarf cypress can be reached by boating or walking along Rose Bay Canal, located on the west side of the lake off State Route 1305. Adjoining the canal is a 153-acre tract of forest that represents the sole surviving stand of virgin timber in the area. Known as Salyer's Ridge Natural Area, the tract includes giant sweetgum, cypress, red maple, and loblolly pine, some reach-ing 90 feet in height and 3 feet in diameter.

Lake Mattamuskeet is crossed by NC 94, and locals can often be seen fishing from the road's shoulders. Common catches in the lake and its canals include catfish, bass, and bream. (Fishing and boating on the lake are prohibited between November 1 and March 1 in order to minimize distur-bance to migratory waterfowl.) "Herring dipping" near an old pumping station—later turned into a visitor's lodge and now a designated national historic site—was once permitted. Tales are told of herring runs so plentiful that people filled the backs of pickup trucks with alewives caught running up the canal into the lake to spawn. Herring dipping is no longer allowed because their numbers have declined so drastically. Efforts are under way to protect and rebuild the remaining herring population.

Another way to explore the lake and its fringes is by canoe. A beautiful and rarely used eight-mile canoe trail begins at the south end of

Previous page: White-tailed deer in a meadow with winter foliage
John Netherton

the lake. It can be accessed at the boat landing along Outfall Canal, near refuge headquarters. Although there are no hiking trails on the refuge, visitors can take a four-mile wildlife drive, which also begins at refuge headquarters. One thing you will not have to worry about out here is crowds. Lake Mattamuskeet is rarely, if ever, overrun with anything but birds.

LOCATION Mattamuskeet National Wildlife Refuge is located in remote eastern North Carolina. To get there, take U.S. 264 east through Swan Quarter and on to the junction with NC 94. Continue north for 1.5 miles to the headquarters entrance road on the right, or turn north on NC 94 to cross Lake Mattamuskeet.

WHEN IT'S OPEN Daily, dawn to dusk. The refuge office is open 7:30 a.m. to 4:00 p.m. on weekdays. Lake Mattamuskeet is closed to fishing and boating from November 1 to March 1.

BEST TIMES TO VISIT Birdwatching is excellent from November to March, when wintering waterfowl occupy the refuge. Fishing in the canals and along the lakeshore is best in spring and fall.

WHAT TO DO Canoeing, birdwatching, wildlife drives, fishing, nature study, and walking along Rose Bay Canal. Three other national wildlife refuges are within a one-hour drive: Swan Quarter, Pocosin Lakes, and Alligator River. In the town of Swanquarter is the landing for the ferry to Ocracoke Island on North Carolina's Outer Banks.

WHERE TO STAY Camping is not permitted in the refuge, but small motels are located near the lake in Fairfield and Engelhard and in the town of Swan Quarter.

FOR MORE INFORMATION Mattamuskeet National Wildlife Refuge, Route 1, Box N-2, Swan Quarter, NC 27885 (919-926-4021).

Merchants Millpond

WETLANDS TYPES:

Cypress-tupelo swamp pond and swamp forest

Duckweed-covered section of millpond
John Netherton

erchants Millpond is one of the most beautiful and out-of-the-way places in North Carolina. It lies off the beaten track in the remote northeast corner of the state, serving as the natural centerpiece of Gates County, with a population of less than 10,000. Set in the midst of rural cotton-growing country, hard by the Virginia border, this approximately 3,100-acre state park is a wilderness lover's paradise. In addition to the 760-acre millpond, there is an ancient cypress-tupelo swamp and a mixed pine-hardwood bottomland forest surrounding it. The millpond and swamp can be explored by canoe, while nine miles of trails traverse the woodlands. Campers can drive to a developed campground, paddle to canoe camps, or hike to backcountry sites.

You will be forgiven for doing a double take upon first laying eyes on Merchants Millpond, which more closely resembles the bayous of Louisiana than the Coastal Plain of North Carolina. The park is very near the northern edge of the range for bald cypress, tupelo gum, and Spanish moss. The latter is the familiar epiphyte found hanging from the stems and branches of trees throughout the Deep South. It might seem out of place this far north, barely 30 miles from the Chesapeake Bay, but nothing about Merchants Millpond and Lassiter Swamp, the associated wetland at its upper end, is very predictable.

You might logically think, for instance, that Merchants Millpond is part of the Great Dismal Swamp, the vast forested bottomland that occupies much of southeastern Virginia and three North Carolina counties. That is not the case. Although the millpond lies only eight miles from the Great Dismal Swamp, it is separated from it by the Suffolk Escarpment and occupies a completely different drainage basin. Instead of flowing east toward the ocean, Bennetts Creek appears to defy nature by moving west through Lassiter Swamp and Merchants Millpond before emptying into the Chowan River. The gently sloping hills surrounding the millpond are another anomaly, creating an environment suitable for plant species more commonly found in the Piedmont (such as trailing arbutus) and trees that thrive in forested uplands (such as American beech).

In the words of park ranger Floyd Williams, "For a person who appreciates diversity in the natural world, this is as good as it gets." The natural bounty at Merchants Millpond is celebrated with ranger-led interpretive programs on most Sundays and some Saturdays. Subjects include snakes, beaver, animal defense mechanisms, and seasonal changes in the swamp.

The millpond and surrounding forest have a rich history as well. Merchants Millpond is 185 years old, having been created when Bennetts

Creek was dammed to power gristmills and sawmills. It was preceded in the early 1700s by Hunters Millpond, built farther upstream. Dam building by beavers also changed the landscape over the centuries.

Beavers were completely eliminated in North Carolina by trappers and those who found the toothy rodent's behavior disruptive to their own land-use plans. However, beavers were reintroduced in North Carolina in the 1970s and gradually made their way into Merchants Millpond. Now, there are 20 to 25 active lodges in the area. The return of beavers has been something of a mixed blessing here and elsewhere in the South. On the positive side, the ponds created by their dams provide habitat for wood ducks, whose numbers have been steadily increasing. On the down side, they have killed off many acres of forested wetlands by flooding them for extended periods—longer than certain impacted bottomland hardwoods can tolerate.

Red skimmer dragonfly, by John Netherton

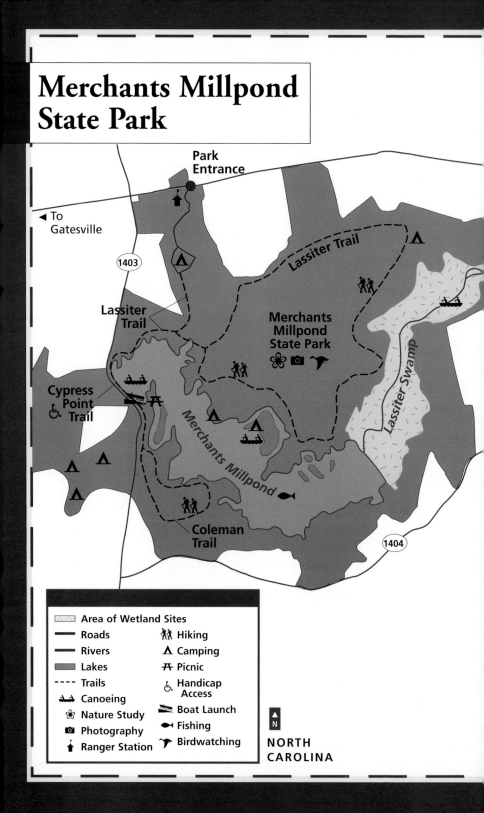

Merchants Millpond State Park

Park Entrance

◄ To Gatesville

1403

Lassiter Trail

Lassiter Trail

Lassiter Swamp

Merchants Millpond State Park

Lassiter Trail

Cypress Point Trail

Merchants Millpond

Coleman Trail

1404

Area of Wetland Sites
Roads
Rivers
Lakes
Trails
Canoeing
Nature Study
Photography
Ranger Station

Hiking
Camping
Picnic
Handicap Access
Boat Launch
Fishing
Birdwatching

N

NORTH CAROLINA

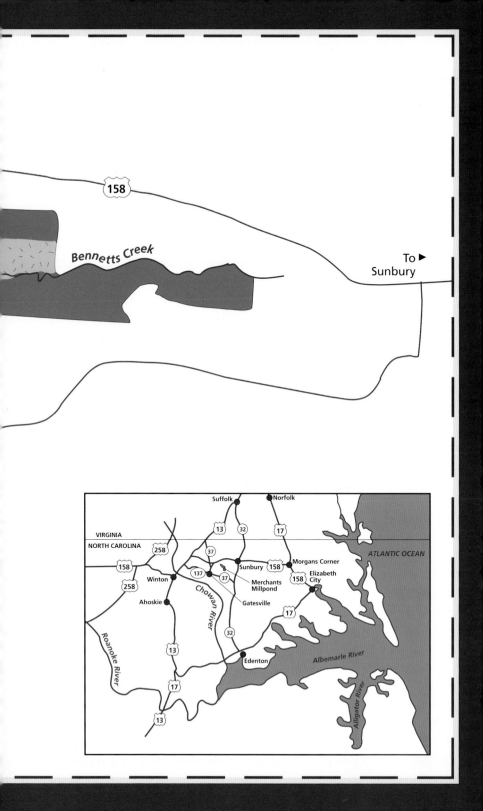

158

Bennetts Creek

To ▶
Sunbury

Suffolk
Norfolk

VIRGINIA
NORTH CAROLINA

13
32
17

258
37

ATLANTIC OCEAN

158
137
Sunbury
158
Morgans Corner

258
Winton
37
Elizabeth
City
158

Merchants
Millpond

Gatesville

Ahoskie
Chowan River
17

Roanoke River
32

13

Edenton
Albemarle River

17

13

Alligator River

A less welcomed park inhabitant is the tick, whose numbers are plentiful from May through September. Common types include dog ticks, deer ticks, and the Lone Star tick, whose larval form is the size of a flake of finely ground pepper. So severe is the tick problem that park managers actually discourage camping in summer. Ticks pose no problem to day-use visitors who come to canoe on the lake, but campers should be aware that the woods are infested with them during warmer months. There are spiders, too, including spectacular orange-bodied, stripe-legged giants that sling heavy-duty webs between trees flanking park trails. Walking face-first into a massive, sticky web with a big, hungry spider for a bull's eye is no picnic.

While close encounters with spiders and ticks come with the territory, park ranger Williams contends that tick-fueled hysteria, driven by fear of Lyme disease and Rocky Mountain spotted fever, has been overstated in this particular geographic area. Having encountered countless bloodsuckers at Merchants Millpond, he offers himself as anecdotal evidence: in 18 years he has never come down with any tick-borne malady. Still, if you plan to visit between Memorial Day and Labor Day, bring a tick-repellent spray or lotion and follow all the usual precautions, including tucking pants into socks, wearing light clothing, and frequently checking for ticks.

Out on the millpond, however, the only nuisance is duckweed. The regrettable preponderance of duckweed mats is the result of non-point source pollution—the technical term for runoff—in this case from agricultural fields and animal lots in the area. Fertilizer and animal wastes are washed out of fields and lots and enter waterways during rainstorms. In still water or on slow-moving lakes and ponds, such as Merchants Millpond, the eutrophic (nutrient-laden) water promotes algal blooms and the growth of duckweed. The pond is especially choked with duckweed at its lower end, near the canoe-rental site. The duckweed forms a thick green skin that looks solid enough to walk on, shading out any submerged aquatic vegetation that might otherwise grow on the pond's bottom, as well as such desirable free-floaters as waterweed, spatterdock (or swampdock), and white water lilies. Duckweed proves an impediment to one's forward progress in a canoe, but farther up the pond it becomes patchier and soon gives way to open water and happy paddling.

The duckweed problem has been exacerbated by a protracted drought that began in March 1994, lowering pond levels and preventing periodic clearing by storms and wind. When the area goes without rain for long periods of time, the next storm rushes a slug of heavily fertilized water from field to stream and into the pond, where it can prove devastating to

White-topped sedge, by John Netherton

aquatic life. One such event in the winter of 1981-82 triggered a rapid bloom, followed by the settling of decaying plant wrack to the bottom, where its consumption raised biological oxygen demand—that is, the demand for oxygen by microorganisms to meet their metabolic requirements. This depletion of oxygen triggered a massive fish kill, and dead fish were removed from the pond by the truckload. "I'm not a trophy fisherman," Williams reflected, "but I saw some bass and other fish pulled out of the pond that people would have given their eye-teeth to catch."

Because duckweed settles to the bottom when it dies, Merchants Millpond is filling in more quickly than it normally would in nature's own time. The visible evidence of eutrophication provided by duckweed is instructional. Even when a wetland is "protected"—as in a state park, for instance—it can be negatively impacted from sources beyond its borders. The lesson is that policy decisions must take into account entire watersheds, not just localized sites. In nature, all is interconnected.

On a positive note, the relatively recent implementation of "best management practices" (BMPs)—procedures for minimizing land runoff and recycling nutrient wastes—on farms and hog lots in Gates County has begun to yield dividends. Williams claims he can already tell a difference on the pond, where he now sees more open space than existed just a few years ago. There are also some improbable positives produced by duckweed's presence. Its shading effect keeps water temperatures cooler in the summer. Because cooler water holds more oxygen, this is beneficial to fish and amphibians. Also, the uptake of nutrient-enriched water enhances the growth of the pond's cypress and gum trees. These are some of the healthiest specimens you will find anywhere. Giant bald cypress and tupelo gums dot the lake, growing more densely as one moves toward Lassiter Swamp. Some are a thousand years old. Even the hollow stumps of dead cypress in the pond are thick with life, their enormous shells serving as planters that support a riot of trees and shrubs, including red maple, sweetgum, wax myrtle, blueberry, and swamp rose.

Fishermen cast for largemouth bass, black crappie, chain pickerel, catfish, bluegill, and sunfish on Merchants Millpond. Such primitive species as bowfin and gar also inhabit the millpond. Wildlife inventories in and around the pond have turned up 202 bird species, 29 fish, 20 snakes, and 10 turtles. One of the more frequent sounds heard on Merchants Millpond is the watery plop of a cooter (pond turtle) as it drops off a log. As the sun falls from sight, other sounds that fill the air out here include the hooting of barred owls and the unearthly screeching of great blue herons.

Longleaf pine bough, by Tom Blagden, Jr.

One of the more splendid experiences on the millpond is canoeing by the light of a silvery moon on a clear evening. With the landscape brightly illuminated by lunar light, you could swear you were paddling through an Ansel Adams photograph. Yet Merchants Millpond is magical at any time of day, whether bathed by the sun's golden rays or on a still, moonlit night. Come prepared to enter an enchanted coastal pond and Southern swamp forest that will take your breath away.

LOCATION Merchants Millpond State Park is located near the community of Gatesville in northeastern North Carolina. Proceed east from Gatesville on U.S. 158 and turn right at State Road 1403 to get to the boathouse and millpond. The park office and campground are located a half mile farther east off U.S. 158; turn right at park entrance sign.

WHEN IT'S OPEN The park office is open from 8:00 a.m. to 4:30 p.m., Monday through Friday. Canoes can be rented from 8:00 a.m. until one hour before closing time.

BEST TIMES TO VISIT The swamp is beautiful year round but is especially so in spring and fall. Avoid coming in summer if you are bothered by heat and ticks.

WHAT TO DO Canoeing (canoes can be rented on-site), camping, hiking, picnicking, fishing, birdwatching, nature study, and interpretive programs.

WHERE TO STAY There is a 20-site family campground near the park office. In addition, Merchants Millpond offers a paddle-in canoe camp with three sites for groups such as scouts, outing clubs, etc. There are also three walk-in group sites. Motels are available 30 miles away in the towns of Elizabeth City, Ahoskie, and Edenton, North Carolina, and Suffolk, Virginia.

FOR MORE INFORMATION Merchants Millpond State Park, Route 1, Box 141A, Gatesville, NC 27938 (919-357-1191).

Turnbull Creek Swamp and Jones Lake

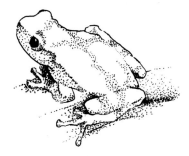

WETLANDS TYPES:

Headwater forest (Turnbull Creek) and
Carolina bay lake (Jones Lake)

Wetland margin of Jones Lake
John Netherton

T urnbull Creek rises in southern Cumberland County and runs through Bladen County before joining the Cape Fear River just east of Elizabethtown. It passes through state forest lands, providing a glimpse of a type of wetland found in the upper reaches of drainage basins. Referred to as a headwater forest or upper perennial riverine wetland, it is less obviously a wetland than, say, a salt marsh or swamp. However, headwater forests serve important functions, such as filtering water and providing food, habitat, and travel corridors for wildlife. This type of forested wetland can be found on upland slopes in mountain, Piedmont, and Coastal Plain locales.

Headwater forests are found along slopes that flank creeks and streams. As water moves downslope, it is intercepted and slowed by trees and vegetation, thus filtering out pollution and sediment from stormwater runoff before it reaches waterways. Soils are often damp and can become saturated near stream channels. Headwater forests generally are not repositories of endangered species, but they are important to a broad cross section of common ones. A variety of trees are found on their slopes, including mockernut hickory, red and white oak, loblolly pine, and blackgum. The understory is composed of various hollies and ferns, as well as greenbrier and poison ivy. Mammalian inhabitants include white-tailed deer, ground squirrels, raccoons, rabbits, and opossums. Seasonal ponds and bogs provide breeding habitat for amphibians.

On the western edge of North Carolina's Coastal Plain, Turnbull Creek is a magical blackwater creek that gurgles rapidly and a bit mysteriously through Bladen County. Visitors can catch sight of it from paths in Turnbull Creek Educational State Forest, particularly on the short, looped Turnbull Creek Trail. On the grounds of this small state forest, 10,000 students a year are introduced to several wetland settings, including a headwater forest, a floodplain swamp, and hillside springs and seeps.

The burbling blackwater of Turnbull Creek snakes its way toward the Cape Fear River, occasionally spilling into small, swampy floodplains when stormwaters flood the creek. One impressive wetland site occupies an inner bend of Turnbull Creek, downhill from the restroom facilities at the Educational State Forest. Plans are to build an observation area and trail along the edge of the swamp, but at present, only those with a truly curious nature (and decent footwear) will want to scramble down the pathless hill to the swamp below. However, it is worth the effort to visit this quiet realm of large trees, snaking vines, and cypress knees. In contrast to the headwater forest on the surrounding hillsides, this is very evidently a wetland—a

Tannin-colored water in Turnbull Creek, by John Netherton

floodplain swamp forest, to be precise. Overflow collects in depressions to the sides of the creek. A mixed stand of water-tolerant hardwoods includes bald cypress, sweetgum, and river birch, with bays, ferns, and holly forming the understory. Cypress knees protrude above the ground. Visitors should note the pronounced difference that 20 feet of elevation makes between the bottomland swamp and upland forest.

One feature of Turnbull Forest that intrigues youthful visitors is its springs and seeps. Water can be seen seeping out of the sides of hills at points along Turnbull Creek Trail. Beavers are active here, and a beaver pond can be viewed just behind the small amphitheater at the head of the trail. The gnawed trunk of a sweetgum stands as mute testimony to the beaver's capacity for destruction. Reindeer moss carpets the ground, and Spanish moss hangs from the trees. Parts of the trail, though seemingly constructed a safe distance from the creek, are inundated several times a year when heavy rains cause flash flooding.

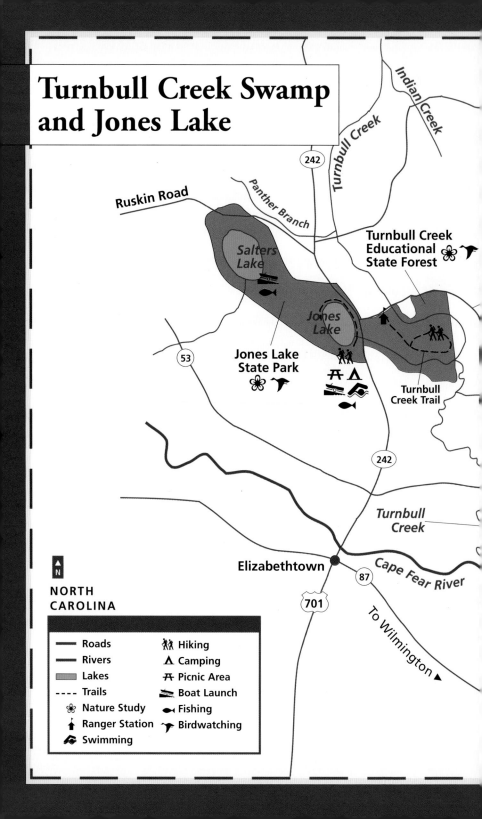

Turnbull Creek Swamp and Jones Lake

Indian Creek

Turnbull Creek

242

Ruskin Road

Panther Branch

Salters Lake

Turnbull Creek Educational State Forest

Jones Lake

53

Jones Lake State Park

Turnbull Creek Trail

242

Turnbull Creek

N

NORTH CAROLINA

Elizabethtown

87

Cape Fear River

701

To Wilmington

▬ Roads	🚶 Hiking
▬ Rivers	⛺ Camping
▭ Lakes	⛱ Picnic Area
---- Trails	🚤 Boat Launch
✿ Nature Study	🎣 Fishing
🚹 Ranger Station	🦆 Birdwatching
🏊 Swimming	

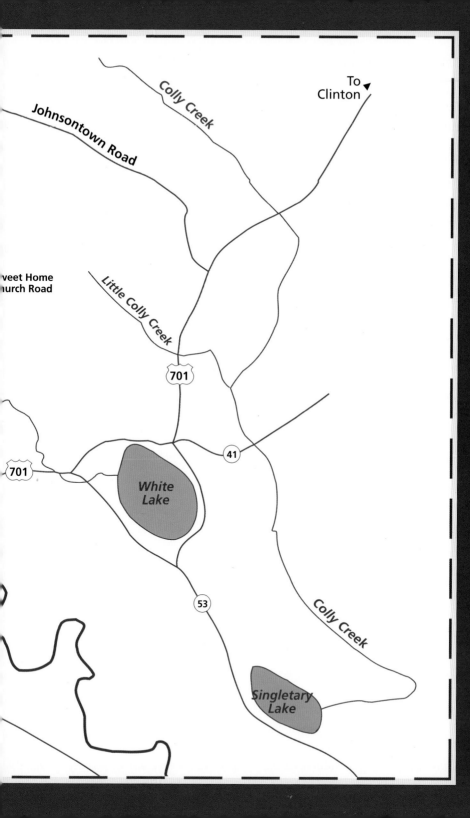

There is still more to see in the way of wetlands. Turnbull Creek lies in the midst of the heaviest concentration of Carolina bay lakes in the South. The tri-county area of Bladen, Columbus, and Cumberland Counties is known as the "bay lakes region" of North Carolina. Singletary, Waccamaw, White, Salters, and Jones Lakes are among the larger and more prominent Carolina bay lakes in the vicinity. Jones Lake lies only a half mile down NC 242 from Turnbull Creek Educational State Forest.

These Carolina bay lakes share some general characteristics: they are oriented from northwest to southeast; they are bounded by a sand rim between one and ten feet in height that is most pronounced at the southeast end; they consist of a sandy bottom that overlies an impermeable clay base; and over time, vegetation invades the lake, causing peat to form over the sandy bottom. Carolina bays are gradually converted to moist bogs, a process of succession that has already consumed many small bay lakes.

At 8,000 feet in length, Jones Lake is one of the larger Carolina bays. Yet today, it is only one-third of its original size. The open-water environment is slowly being invaded from its margins by hydrophilic (water-tolerant) trees and shrubs, including three well-known "bays"— sweetbay, redbay, and loblolly bay—so named because of their affinity for the shorelines of Carolina bays.

Jones Lake is relatively shallow (with an average depth of 8.7 feet) and tannic (tea-colored, due to the decomposition of organic material). By contrast, White Lake—another bay lake in the vicinity—is clear. The sugar-white sand that rims the bay lakes and whitens the landscape was deposited in ancient times when the area was covered by an inland sea. Swimming at Jones Lake State Park—whose facilities include a bathhouse and a pier—is a bit like a day at the beach, with sand, sun, and cool, inviting water. Rowboats can be rented, and a three-mile nature trail encircles the lake. Wetlands enthusiasts will enjoy exploring the bay-bog community surrounding the lake, which includes Atlantic white cedar, sweetgum and blackgum, pond pine, loblolly pine, and bald cypress in the canopy. The aforementioned bay species form the midstory, while understory vegetation includes gallberry, fetterbush, pepperbush, and insectivorous Venus flytraps and pitcher-plants.

For the truly adventurous visitor, Jones Lake State Park incorporates another Carolina bay lake within its boundaries—Salters Lake. This lake (315 acres) is almost half again as large as Jones Lake (224 acres). Access to it, however, is restricted and permission must be obtained at the park office. After you have filled out a form, a park ranger will escort you to a locked gate and direct you to Salters Lake. A two-mile drive down a sandy, cratered back road deposits you at the lip of a pristine, expansive lake that is yours to enjoy in a rowboat, canoe, or motorboat. A boat launch, framed by bald cypress, lies at the end of the road.

LOCATION Turnbull Creek Educational State Forest and Jones Lake State Park are located four miles north of Elizabethtown on NC 242.

WHEN IT'S OPEN Turnbull Creek Educational State Forest is open from mid-March to mid-November, Monday through Friday from 8:00 a.m. to 5:00 p.m. and Saturday from 9:00 a.m. to 5:00 p.m. Jones Lake State Park opens at 8:00 a.m. all year and closes at 6:00 p.m. from November through February; 7:00 p.m. in March and October; 8:00 p.m. in April, May, and September; and 9:00 p.m. from June through August.

BEST TIMES TO VISIT The fall months bring an array of bright colors to the trees of Turnbull Creek Educational State Forest. The summer months are an opportune time to cool off in Jones Lake.

WHAT TO DO At Turnbull Creek Educational State Forest, hiking, picnicking, ranger-conducted programs, and nature study can be enjoyed. Nine educational programs related to forest uses and aimed at elementary school groups are led by forest rangers. Call (910-588-4161) to schedule a visit.

At Jones Lake State Park, swimming, hiking, boating, fishing, camping, picnicking, and birdwatching are popular activities.

WHERE TO STAY There are 20 wooded campsites at Jones Lake State Park. There are also motels in Elizabethtown, four miles away.

FOR MORE INFORMATION Turnbull Creek Educational State Forest, 4506 NC 242 North, Elizabethtown, NC 28337 (910-588-4161); Jones Lake State Park, 113 Jones Lake Drive, Elizabethtown, NC 28337 (910-588-4550).

SOUTH CAROLINA

ACE Basin

WETLANDS TYPES:

Varied freshwater, saltwater, and brackish wetlands

Tickseed flowers on the Ashepoo River
Tom Blagden, Jr.

T he ACE Basin is the pearl of South Carolina's low country. It is an amazing network of wetlands and associated uplands that occupies 350,000 acres of wilderness along the southern coast of the state. Its preservation is no less amazing—a feat of multi-party planning and cooperation. Since the ACE Basin Task Force was formed in 1988, great strides have been made in bringing together diverse interests—private landowners, timber companies, duck hunters, government agencies, and environmental groups—to find common cause in formulating a long-range plan to protect and preserve the natural splendor of the ACE Basin. The immediate and ongoing success of this ambitious, ecosystem-wide endeavor has drawn attention from all over the world and provided a blueprint for future strategies on how to manage wetland ecosystems.

First, let us take a look at the ACE Basin. "ACE" is an acronym of the three rivers that empty into St. Helena Sound on the lower South Carolina coast: the Ashepoo, the Combahee, and the Edisto. They are black-water streams—so named for the tea-colored stain imparted by the tannins that leach out of decaying plant material—that lazily meander across the Coastal Plain. The Edisto River is the longest and largest. It is, in fact, one of the longest blackwater rivers in the country, rolling for 300 miles from its headwaters near Aiken. The Edisto and its associated bottomlands form the basin's northern boundary, passing around marshy Edisto Island before entering the Atlantic Ocean. The middle river in the system is the Ashepoo. Forming the southern boundary, the Combahee is considered the most scenic, harboring dramatic swamp forests that include spectacular bald cypress stands. From their distant origins across the state, the three rivers nearly converge at the coastal margin of the basin, entering St. Helena Sound within seven miles of each other.

The inland boundary of the ACE Basin is U.S. 17A; the city of Charleston lies 45 miles to the northeast. The area seaward of the highway between the three rivers is a majestic, varied landscape that takes in a plethora of wetlands: cypress-gum swamps, bottomland hardwood forests, freshwater marshes, salt marshes, brackish tidal marshes, interior ponds, and more. Also interesting, from a wetlands perspective, are the manmade impoundments that have created thousands of acres of freshwater marsh throughout the ACE Basin. The surprising fact is that they were not designed for this purpose in recent decades, but are historical relics of a time when the area was cleared of trees, ditched, and diked for rice planting. The same water management structures that worked to make the low country of South Carolina the nation's primary supplier of rice in the 1700s and 1800s is now used to nurture freshwater wetlands that are managed for migratory waterfowl and other wetland wildlife.

Modern techniques for waterfowl habitat management involve using water from flooding tidal creeks to overflow the fields through water-control structures that have been adapted without refinement from the days of the rice planters. These techniques have been successfully employed throughout the ACE Basin, including portions of the 11,000 acres managed as a national wildlife refuge. Numerous species of waterfowl, as well as other birds and wildlife species, use refuge impoundments. Many common marsh plants, including bladderwort, soft rush, smartweed, cattail, and swamp loosestrife, are found on these flooded fields. Wigeongrass and other waterfowl food plants are cultivated in brackish managed wetlands. It is, incidentally, hard to escape the legacy of rice planting in the area. Two of the primary agencies managing the ACE Basin—The Nature Conservancy and the U.S. Fish and Wildlife Service—are jointly headquartered at Grove Plantation, a rice grower's mansion that dates from 1828.

The ACE Basin provides critical habitat for 16 endangered and rare species. Among them are bald eagles and wood storks, which have made stunning comebacks in the basin. Between 1981 and 1995, the wood stork —the only stork native to North America—increased from 11 to 651 nesting pairs. More are arriving all the time from South Florida, where their habitat is dwindling. Loggerhead turtles—a threatened species—inhabit the off-shore waters and nest on barrier islands in the basin. The population of the formerly endangered American alligator has exploded, with the slithering reptiles being able to find ample food in the shallows while building banks that serve as nesting sites on the high marsh. Gray and fox squirrels, rabbits, and raccoons are common. Bobcats, river otters, and mink also occupy the basin. Game species include deer, wild turkey, quail, mourning doves, and snipe.

Such species diversity has been maintained here largely because the ACE Basin has remained in the hands of a small number of private landowners who espouse a conservation ethic and do not want to see the essential character of their beloved low country altered. Their willingness to sign conservation easements, combined with the efforts of government agencies and nonprofit conservation groups to buy land in the basin as it becomes available, has yielded extraordinary results.

To date, 125,000 acres within the ACE Basin—nearly a third of its total area, including some of the most sensitive and significant wetlands —have been protected from future development, either through outright acquisition or conservation easements. The latter is a legal document whereby

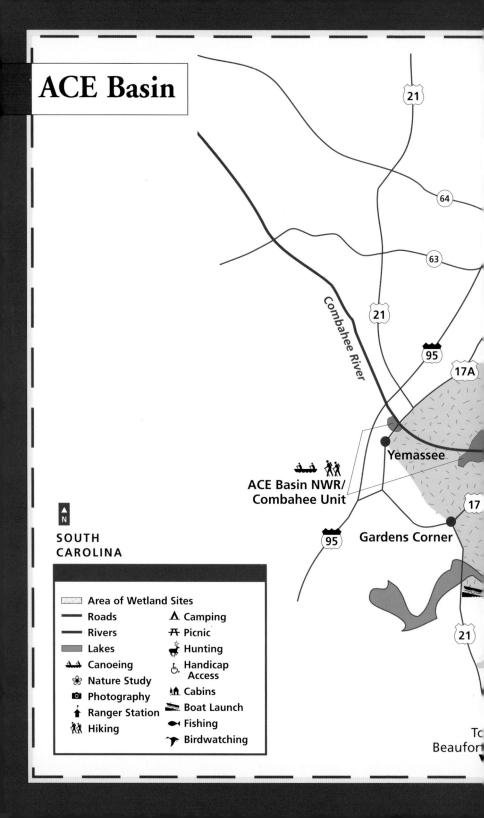

ACE Basin

21

64

63

Combahee River

21

95

17A

ᴥᴥᴥ 🏃‍➕ Yemassee

ACE Basin NWR/
Combahee Unit

17

95 Gardens Corner

21

▲
N

SOUTH
CAROLINA

Area of Wetland Sites	
— Roads	▲ Camping
— Rivers	🎋 Picnic
Lakes	🦌 Hunting
ᴥᴥᴥ Canoeing	♿ Handicap Access
❀ Nature Study	🏚 Cabins
📷 Photography	🚤 Boat Launch
♠ Ranger Station	➤ Fishing
🏃 Hiking	🦅 Birdwatching

To
Beaufort

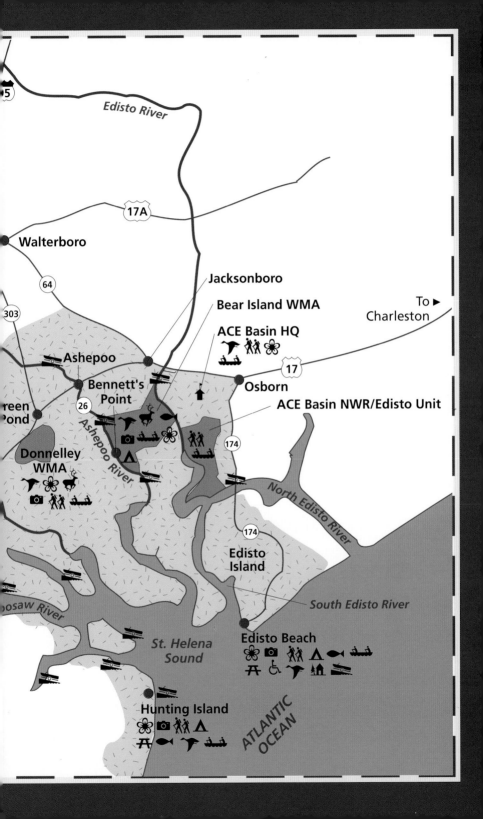

landowners voluntarily place a permanent easement or deed restriction on their property that forbids certain uses, such as industrial, commercial, or multi-family development, in order to preserve the habitat integrity of the basin.

Through such mechanisms, the preservation of areas like the ACE Basin can be achieved without condemning land. The strategy of making partners and not adversaries of private landowners was written into the statement of objectives drafted by the ACE Basin Task Force in 1988. The principal agencies responsible for the ACE Basin Habitat Protection and Enhancement Plan are The Nature Conservancy, Ducks Unlimited, the U.S. Fish and Wildlife Service, and the South Carolina Department of Natural Resources. More than 60 other organizations and agencies support conservation efforts in the ACE Basin as well. Such creative partnerships hold much promise for future wetlands preservation and restoration undertakings.

Unlike other wetlands described in this publication, the major portion of the land in the ACE Basin remains under private ownership. The rice plantations have changed hands over generations but have not been subdivided, so the land looks much as it did a century or two ago. To date, those areas that have been acquired by government or conservation groups have been managed for wildlife, with efforts under way to develop public access. To put it all into perspective, the ACE Basin is not a park but an ecosystem.

Although visitors cannot readily explore the whole of the ACE Basin, there are ways to experience the essence of the basin's diverse habitat. The easiest and best means is by car. Secondary roads pass through Donnelley and Bear Island Wildlife Management Areas, which are crossed by all three rivers as they near the ocean. The best point of entry into the basin is at the intersection of U.S. 17 and SC 26 (Bennett's Point Road), seven miles south of Jacksonboro. Bennett's Point Road penetrates the basin for 16 miles, paralleling and then crossing the Ashepoo River before dead-ending at Mosquito Creek, one of the Ashepoo's tributaries, by Bennett's Point Landing.

The bridge over the Ashepoo is a superb place to survey a vast expanse of brackish marsh. Black needlerush dominates the river's margins, yielding to mixed forests of oak, pine, wax myrtle, and palmetto (South Carolina's state tree). This entire area is managed for wintering waterfowl by the state. Fall and winter visitors include sizable flocks of ducks (including pintails and mallards), geese, and tundra swans. They are joined by bald eagles, wood storks, ospreys, egrets, herons, anhingas, and many others. Two miles

Previous page: Aerial view of salt marsh on the Combahee River
Tom Blagden, Jr.

Black skimmer, by Tom Blagden, Jr.

beyond the bridge is the entrance to Bear Island WMA headquarters, from which vantage point you can view waterfowl and wildlife, including alligators, in the impoundments. Three miles farther, at the end of the road, you can look out across the boat landing in the direction of the ACE Basin Natural Estuarine Reserve, a complex of low-lying islands crosshatched with tidal creeks that twice daily pump seawater into areas dominated by stands of salt-tolerant *Spartina alterniflora* (salt marsh cordgrass).

From Bennett's Point, backtrack along SC 26 until it rejoins U.S. 17, and then proceed south for 3.7 miles. Turn left on SC 161, "Dirt Wiggins Road," a 5-mile dirt road that passes some magnificent old live oaks draped in Spanish moss and resurrection ferns. The mixed hardwood forest, which includes some sizable hickories, warrants an appreciative stop or two along this rarely traveled back road. Dirt Wiggins Road soon meets SC 162, "Paved Wiggins Road." A short distance past this junction lies Old Chehaw River Boat Landing. It is well worth making the short lefthand detour to this spot, which is one of the most serene and scenic settings in the ACE Basin.

Back on SC 162, continue for six more miles until the road gives out at Field's Point Boat Landing. It is located on the Combahee River, several miles before its waters mingle with those of the Coosaw River at the head of St. Helena Sound. The short bluffs above the boat landing, shaded by live oaks, make a terrific picnic spot. On the return trip out to U.S. 17, stay on SC 162, "Paved Wiggins Road," the entire way, and you will see a bit more of the basin.

Hiking opportunities in the basin are limited but will surely increase in coming years. Two trails—the mile-long Edisto Nature Trail and the 3.1-mile Bluff Trail—are maintained on 17,000 acres of forest owned by Westvaco, a lumber company that has committed itself to responsible stewardship of its holdings in the basin. Within Donnelley Wildlife Management Area is Boynton Nature Trail, a 2.2-mile hike that wanders past swamp forests and marshy impoundments. Visitors can also hike within the ACE Basin National Wildlife Refuge; drop by refuge headquarters for maps and information. Kayaking and canoeing offer the most revealing look at the basin. A local outfitter—Life Quest Adventures, located at the junction of U.S. 17 and the Ashepoo River—rents kayaks and canoes and offers guided tours of the ACE Basin.

You can also tour the ACE Basin from an armchair via Tom Blagden, Jr.'s exquisite book of photography, *South Carolina's Wetland Wilderness: The ACE Basin* (Westcliffe Publishers, 1992). His images say volumes about the majesty of wetlands and the diversity of life forms they harbor. It is a tribute worthy of the ACE Basin, whose priceless beauty warrants everlasting preservation.

LOCATION The ACE Basin is a 350,000-acre "wetlands wilderness" formed by the Ashepoo, Combahee, and Edisto Rivers seaward of U.S. 17A. The basin is centered 45 miles southwest of Charleston and is roughly outlined by a crescent formed by the towns of Yemassee, Walterboro, and Jacksonboro.

Brochures, maps, and information can be obtained at ACE Basin National Wildlife Refuge headquarters. To get there, turn onto SC 174 from its junction with U.S. 17, 6 miles east of Jacksonboro (26 miles southwest of Charleston). Follow SC 174 for 2 miles through Adams Run, then turn right on Willtown Road (SC 55) and follow signs to refuge headquarters, which is located in Grove Plantation.

Previous page: White ibis at Bear Island Wildlife Management Area
Tom Blagden, Jr.

The office for Donnelley Wildlife Management Area is open 8:00 a.m. to 5:00 p.m., Monday through Friday. To get there, turn right off U.S. 17 immediately north of its junction with SC 303 and follow the dirt road to the park office. Visitor registration is requested, and maps and information are available.

The Westvaco Company's Timberlands Division maintains two public trails: Edisto Nature Trail, at U.S. 17 just east of Jacksonboro, and Bluff Trail, located 13 miles south of Walterboro at the junction of U.S. 17A and SC 66. Visits to the latter are by appointment only and there is no charge; call Westvaco's South Areas office (803-538-8353) from 8:00 a.m. to 5:00 p.m. on weekdays.

Life Quest Adventures, a private outfitter specializing in outdoor adventures in the ACE Basin, is located in Green Pond where U.S. 17 meets the Ashepoo River; call (803-844-8877) for reservations and information.

WHEN IT'S OPEN Public roads through the ACE Basin can, of course, be driven at any time. The ACE Basin National Wildlife Refuge headquarters is open Monday through Friday, 7:30 a.m. to 4:00 p.m., except on holidays. Donnelley Wildlife Management Area, site of the Boynton Nature Trail, is open for wildlife observation, birdwatching, photography, hiking, and nature study from 8:00 a.m. to 5:00 p.m., Monday through Saturday, except during scheduled public hunts (call ahead for dates) and from November 1 through January 21 to minimize disturbance to migratory waterfowl.

BEST TIMES TO VISIT Spring for greenery and wildflowers, late fall and winter for birdwatching.

WHAT TO DO Driving tours, hiking, fishing, hunting, picnicking, birdwatching, canoeing and kayaking, and nature study.

WHERE TO STAY There are no places to camp in the ACE Basin. Motels abound at the Walterboro and Yemassee exits off I-95.

FOR MORE INFORMATION ACE Basin National Wildlife Refuge, P.O. Box 848, Hollywood, SC 29449 (803-889-3084); Donnelley Wildlife Management Area, 585 Donnelley Drive, Green Pond, SC 29446 (803-844-8957).

Carolina Sandhills National Wildlife Refuge

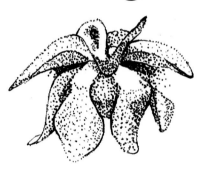

WETLANDS TYPES:

Seepage bogs, lake/pond fringe, riparian bottomland hardwoods

Green tree frog on underside of a leaf
John Netherton

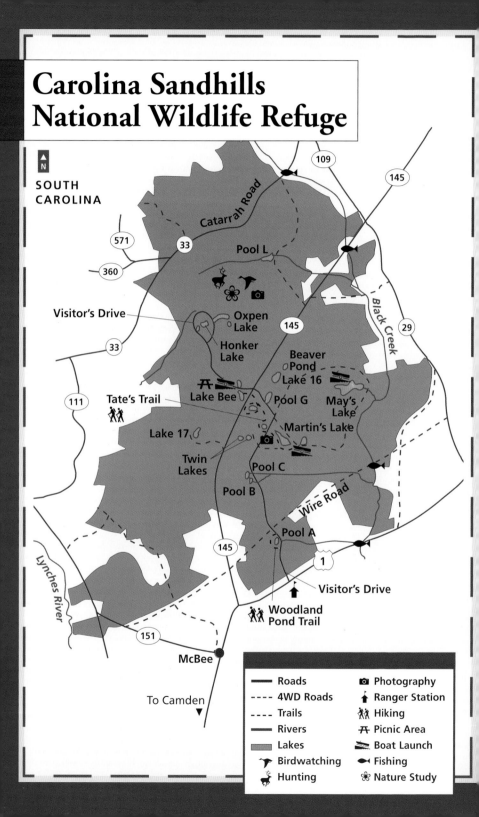

Carolina Sandhills National Wildlife Refuge

N

SOUTH CAROLINA

571
33
360

109
145

Catarrah Road

Pool L

Visitor's Drive
Oxpen Lake
145
Honker Lake
33

Beaver Pond
Lake 16
Black Creek
29

111
Tate's Trail
Lake Bee
Pool G
May's Lake

Lake 17
Martin's Lake

Twin Lakes
Pool C
Pool B

Wire Road

Pool A
1

Visitor's Drive

Woodland Pond Trail

Lynches River

151
McBee

To Camden

—— Roads	📷 Photography
- - - - 4WD Roads	🚹 Ranger Station
- - - Trails	🚶 Hiking
—— Rivers	🎋 Picnic Area
▮ Lakes	🛶 Boat Launch
🐦 Birdwatching	◀ Fishing
🦌 Hunting	❀ Nature Study

arolina Sandhills National Wildlife Refuge extends over 46,000 acres and is home to a rich assortment of plant and animal life, including rare and endangered species. It is an area of sandy uplands, spring-fed streams, and boggy bottomlands located in northeastern South Carolina. This belt of rolling sandhills—relict dunes that date from 55 million years ago, a time when the Atlantic Ocean extended this far inland—continues into North Carolina and the popular resorts of Pinehurst and Southern Pines. Carolina Sandhills National Wildlife Refuge straddles the fall line—the hilly, transitional zone between the Piedmont Plateau and the Coastal Plain. The soils are mainly deep beds of sand, with some organic soil accumulation in the boggy depressions and on hillsides.

Wetland sites abound on the refuge, which has been managed for waterfowl through the creation of 30 manmade lakes and ponds. Emergent grasses that grow on the impoundments serve as food sources for ducks and geese. There are many migratory species that overwinter on the refuge, although some wood ducks and Canada geese are present all year. Bottomlands along the creeks support stands of mixed hardwoods, while the sandhills give rise to pine-scrub oak communities. A drive through the refuge reveals extensive tracts of spindly longleaf pines with a dense turkey oak understory.

The sandhills are in the process of reverting to the longleaf pine/red-cockaded woodpecker ecosystem that represents the climax state to which the area had progressed in pre-settlement times. The land was heavily logged and farmed, leading to erosion, barrenness, and the almost total elimination of wildlife. In 1939, the refuge was purchased by the government under the Resettlement Act and has since been restored through sound conservation so that it once again is a healthy environment for plants and wildlife. Today, Carolina Sandhills supports the largest population of red-cockaded woodpeckers—more than a hundred colonies—of any refuge in the country. These birds are very particular about where they nest, preferring living, mature, longleaf pines afflicted with red-heart disease—a fungus that softens the heartwood, enabling the woodpeckers to hollow out cavities for nesting purposes.

Those who come to Carolina Sandhills to see wetlands will be rewarded with pond, lake, creekside, and bottomland sites, as well as the refuge's renowned seepage bogs. Observation towers on Oxpen Lake and Martin's Lake afford opportunities for wildlife study, especially from December through February. At this time, migrating ducks and geese inhabit the refuge in large numbers. A brochure available at refuge headquarters lists all of the bird species that have been sighted on the refuge—a 208-item inventory that ranges from sandpipers to sapsuckers and coots to canvasbacks.

Sundew, by Tom Blagden, Jr.

Two nature trails follow the edges of several lakes and ponds. The Woodland Pond Trail makes a one-mile loop around Pool A, while Tate's Trail runs for two miles between Lake Bee and Martin's Lake (necessitating a return trip of equal length). Woodland Pond Trail crosses a small, sandy-bottomed creek at the point where it enters Pool A, which is in the process of being colonized from the margins by water-tolerant trees, shrubs, and vines. Some of the trees in these woodlands and wetlands are blackgum and sweetgum, water and willow oak, tulip poplar, white cedar, and pond cypress. The path then ascends to a pine-scrub oak upland whose floor is carpeted with longleaf pine needles that are a foot or more in length, as well as massive pine cones.

If you want to see more of the sandhills than these short trails allow, a hundred miles of mostly unpaved roads—plus an eight-mile paved Visitor's Drive—wind through the reserve. These roads are generally open to the public, although some environmentally sensitive areas are off-limits. Also, several brief hunting seasons may affect accessibility. Call the refuge office for dates and details of restricted access and closures.

Seepage bogs are a rare and limited wetland type scattered throughout the Carolina Sandhills. They are found on slopes where the water table comes to the surface, resulting in ground seepage. Because of the unique community these wetlands support, the public is discouraged from walking on them. Roads leading to the larger sites are generally gated. They are, and deserve to remain, untrampled. However, groups with an interest in wetlands may call to request a supervised visit.

Previous page: Water-tolerant trees along Martin's Lake
Tom Blagden, Jr.

These seepage bogs remain wet year-round. They are covered with grasses and shrubs, so their boggy nature is not evident unless you walk across them. Indeed, beneath the herbaceous layer lies a nutrient-poor but organic-rich muck that supports a plant community not dissimilar to a North Carolina pocosin. (Think of it as a pocosin on a slope instead of in a depression.) There are an estimated 200 acres of seepage bogs in the refuge and close to 600 individual sites, some of which are very small. The acidic bogs give rise to small evergreen shrubs such as sweetbay. Further evidence of nutrient-poor soil is the presence of sundews and pitcher-plants—plants that rely on insects as a source of vital nutrients lacking in the soil. They work by trapping and digesting insects. The sundew, for example, has leaves tipped with sticky glands that ensnare insects. Three varieties of pitcher-plant are found on the reserve, all of them designed to entrap, drown, and digest their unsuspecting prey. Light surface fires tend to promote the growth and spread of pitcher-plants, and the bogs are periodically burned to rejuvenate the groundcover and prevent woody vegetation from taking root.

The most noteworthy resident in the refuge is the Pine Barrens tree frog. This striking amphibian lives in the bogs and breeds in its streamlets. Colored bright green with a purple stripe, this racy-looking frog is confined to scattered pockets between New Jersey and South Carolina and is listed as a threatened species. The Carolina Sandhills seepage bogs, which provide habitat for numerous species, both rare and common, are a striking example of how wetlands serve as living laboratories of adaptation and evolution.

LOCATION Carolina Sandhills National Wildlife Refuge is located four miles northeast of McBee on U.S. 1.

WHEN IT'S OPEN The refuge is open during daylight hours all year. The office is open from 8:00 a.m. to 4:30 p.m. on weekdays.

BEST TIMES TO VISIT April-May and September-October for the best birdwatching.

WHAT TO DO Birdwatching, fishing, hunting, picnicking, nature walks and drives, and nature study.

WHERE TO STAY Camping is prohibited on the refuge, but there is a developed campground at Cheraw State Park, 25 miles north of refuge headquarters on U.S. 1. Motels are available in the town of McBee, four miles away.

FOR MORE INFORMATION Carolina Sandhills National Wildlife Refuge, Route 2, Box 330, McBee, SC 29101 (803-335-8401).

Congaree Swamp

WETLANDS TYPES:

Redwater bottomland hardwood swamp

Bald cypress at Wise Lake
Tom Blagden, Jr.

T he Congaree Swamp is a wetland for the record books. It consti-
tutes the largest remaining stand of old-growth forest in the East.
It is the largest tract of climax swamp forest in the entire United
States. At one time, the Congaree was the site of 9 national and
24 state champion trees. (A champion tree is the largest on record for a given
species, based on circumference, height, and canopy.) Having largely been
spared the logging fate that befell nearly every other virgin stand in the East
during this nation's clearcutting frenzy, the Congaree survives as a living
museum of tall trees. They have been called "the redwoods of the East."

The swamp is located in the floodplain of the Congaree River,
which is formed by the confluence of the Saluda and Broad Rivers and runs
for 60 miles, losing its identity when it flows into the Wateree. The swamp
lies 17 miles east of Columbia and about 1,000 years from the sawing hands
of civilization. Some of the trees and stumps in the Congaree's 11,000 acres of
virgin timber were already ancient when Columbus arrived. A count of one
particularly prodigious cypress stump yielded 1,700 annual rings.

There are even massive old loblolly pines in the Congaree. Never
mind that elsewhere they rarely live for more than a hundred years. Loblolly
pines thrive here, surviving for as many as 300 years and reaching heights of
160 feet. It has been theorized that an extended period of drought, followed
by fire, opened up the forest floor to colonization by loblolly seedlings at
several different times in the past. Whatever the reason, it adds to the eternal
mystery of the Congaree Swamp.

The floodplain of the Congaree ranges from between three and five
miles in width, with the uncut portion of the swamp extending for six miles
along the river. The floodplain is situated north of the river, with the high
bluffs of Calhoun County rising from the south bank. (At the same time that
grassroots groups were petitioning to save Congaree Swamp, the contrary-
minded government of Calhoun County passed a law prohibiting the sale of
land in the county to the National Park Service!) It is the broad floodplain
that is preserved as the Congaree Swamp National Monument. The swamp
was established as a preserve with an initial purchase of 15,000 acres in 1976.
The National Park Service arrived in 1978. Ten years later, an additional
7,000 acres was purchased, providing high ground to which animals could
escape in times of flooding. Today, Congaree Swamp is celebrated as an example
of "nature at its best" (according to *National Geographic*) and has been accorded
the status of an International Biosphere Reserve (by the United Nations).

Visitors to Congaree Swamp can choose from 20 miles of trails
or paddle an 18-mile canoe trail that runs along Cedar Creek (the largest

Green tree frog, by John Netherton

channel on the floodplain) and the Congaree River. For those who want to experience up-close a classic cypress-tupelo swamp without getting their feet wet, the low boardwalk that runs for 0.6 mile is an unforgettable passage. Constructed barely inches above the inundated floodplain, the boardwalk wanders through a giant, cathedral-like stand of bald cypress and water tupelo. Cypress knees—conical protrusions from the trees' root systems that provide stability and allow for gas exchange—stick out of the water. Where stationary, the water has the dark, tannic color typical of blackwater swamps. Where it flows or is unsettled, the water is muddy and opaque, resembling coffee with cream. That is because the Congaree carries a significant volume of silt and clay in suspension, depositing its reddish, milky overflow onto the floodplain. Vegetation in low-lying areas has a sallow, grayish-green cast from regular drenchings with muddy water. According to park officials, 95 percent of the park is under water at least five times a year. For this reason, it is a good idea to call ahead and check conditions before visiting.

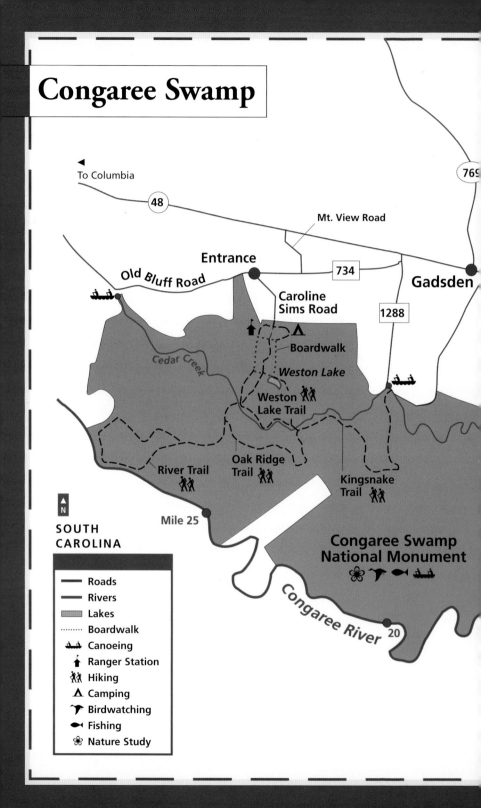

Congaree Swamp

◀ To Columbia

(48)

Mt. View Road

769

Entrance

Old Bluff Road

734

Gadsden

Caroline Sims Road

1288

Cedar Creek

Boardwalk

Weston Lake

Weston Lake Trail

River Trail

Oak Ridge Trail

Kingsnake Trail

Mile 25

N

SOUTH CAROLINA

Congaree Swamp National Monument

Congaree River

20

⎯⎯	Roads
⎯⎯	Rivers
▨	Lakes
·······	Boardwalk
🛶	Canoeing
⛢	Ranger Station
🚶	Hiking
Λ	Camping
⏚	Birdwatching
◀━	Fishing
❀	Nature Study

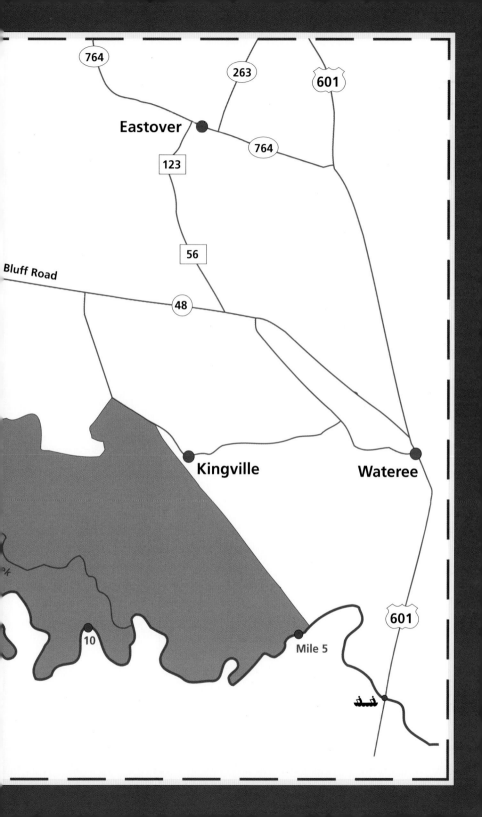

The counterpart to the low boardwalk is the elevated boardwalk, a stilted walkway that runs above a drier section of old-growth forest, ending at a deck that overlooks Weston Lake. Located on a slightly higher section of floodplain that is subjected to periodic, as opposed to constant, inundation, the forest crossed by this boardwalk harbors such water-tolerant trees and shrubs as water oak, laurel oak, tulip poplar, ironwood, sweetgum, red maple, redbay, and sweetbay. Regularly fertilized by the nutrient-laden waters of the Congaree, the trees and shrubs grow to unusual heights here. Pawpaws are a common understory tree in many sections of the park. Visitors should be wary of poison sumac, whose toxic sap can cause an extremely bothersome and persistent rash.

The two boardwalks are joined by a connector trail to form a circuit hike from the visitor center that runs slightly under three miles. Other trails in the Congaree system roam the ridges and swales of the backcountry floodplain at ground level, which means that you will almost certainly get your feet wet. The Oak Ridge Trail crosses numerous small creeks and hardwood flats. The River Trail eventually reaches and then runs alongside the Congaree River for more than a mile. The latter is an all-day hike for those wanting to set off early from the visitor center and return before dark. Backcountry camping is an alternative. (Obtain permits at the visitor center.) Waterproof footgear and a willingness to slog through muddy and watery stretches are certainly prerequisites for hiking beyond the boardwalks. At one point during a long hike undertaken by this writer the day after a heavy rain, the Oak Ridge Trail disappeared under a foot of water for a few hundred feet, requiring some enterprising guesswork (and a little blind luck) to recover its course. But that is all part of the adventure.

The hydrology of the Congaree Swamp is a virtual primer on the structure and function of floodplains. The Congaree is part of a watershed that drains 40 percent of the state of South Carolina. It meanders across the Coastal Plain, with numerous small tributaries and a main channel (Cedar Creek) draining into it. Oxbow lakes, such as Weston Lake, are remnants of old meanders that were cut off when the river took a straighter course. In this way, what was once a bend in the river became a narrow, U-shaped lake. Weston Lake, a spring-fed oxbow, has persisted for 10,000 years.

During storm periods, the river rises and the flow in the Congaree's floodplain tributaries actually changes direction. At these times, water flows

Previous page: Sunrise from bluffs of the Congaree River
Tom Blagden, Jr.

out of the main river into its branch creeks, and the overflow is distributed across the floodplain. In its water-storage function, the Congaree Swamp acts as a natural form of flood control. The water is held in depressions, absorbed by the ground, and taken up by trees and vegetation—an efficient system for processing overflow that effectively prevents downstream flooding while supporting a unique ecosystem of trees and shrubs adapted to periodic inundation.

The Congaree Swamp is home to 320 plant species, including 90 different kinds of trees. Although the elevation change across the floodplain is slight, it is enough to support markedly different ecological associations. Each species possesses a varied tolerance for exposure to standing water and therefore claims relatively higher or lower areas within the swamp. The area is also rich in fauna, sheltering 24 reptile, 41 mammal, 52 fish, and 200 bird species. Congaree Swamp is a birder's paradise.

So just how did this majestic swamp escape the logging fate that befell so many of South Carolina's virgin forests? Through the conservationist convictions of a lumberman, as unlikely as that may sound. Timber company magnate Francis Beidler owned sizable tracts of land in South Carolina, including the Congaree Swamp. Fortunately, he made providential visits to Yellowstone National Park in Wyoming and Yosemite National Park in California. Overcome by the great beauty of the West, he saw a similar value in the old-growth forest of the Congaree Swamp. Although he logged his other holdings, he spared Congaree Swamp and Four Holes Swamp (see separate entry), two of the more awe-inspiring locales in the state. It was not until the land passed to his grandchildren that the old-growth forest of the Congaree was threatened by cutting. Logging began in the 1960s and proceeded at the rate of up to a thousand acres per year. A hue and cry from the public, led by a vocal grassroots coalition, successfully set in motion the purchase from the Beidler heirs of the still-untouched heart of the Congaree Swamp.

You might think the story would end here, with the "redwoods of the East" living happily ever after. But then nature itself threw the Congaree Swamp a curve ball by hurtling one of the most powerful storms of the century, Hurricane Hugo, through the area on its destructive path between Charleston and Charlotte in September 1989. What no timber company had done in a century, Hugo accomplished in one night, felling some of the Congaree Swamp's tallest timber.

The shallow-rooted trees of swamps and bottomlands are particularly susceptible to high winds, and Hugo wiped out 25 percent of the trees and

Red maples in Congaree Swamp, by Tom Blagden, Jr.

50 percent of the canopy in Congaree Swamp. A national champion Shumard oak (20 feet in circumference and 155 feet tall, with a canopy that spread 116 feet) was downed. A former national champion overcup oak toppled as well. The bigger they were, the harder they fell. The remains of these gentle giants litter the forest floor. Their massive root systems were ripped from the ground and now stand vertically with 150 feet or more of dead trunk extended behind them. But they will not remain in this condition for long. In the humid, temperate climate of the Congaree, trees decompose to soil in eight years or less.

The National Park Service, which takes a laissez-faire approach to nature's doings, has allowed the forest to regenerate without interference. Although the aftermath of Hugo seems almost horrifically tragic, there is a silver lining to this dark cloud. By opening up the canopy, more light can now reach the forest floor; this has allowed new seedlings to colonize and provide grazing areas for wildlife. All 200 bird species previously inventoried at Congaree Swamp have been sighted since the hurricane. Birdwatchers have reported increased sightings of the indigo bunting, the Kentucky warbler, the Louisiana waterthrush, Swainson's warbler, and the Eastern wood pewee. In addition, the woodpecker population in the swamp has increased significantly in the wake of Hugo.

Consequently, it is important to recognize the role that catastrophism plays in nature. One reason huge trees exist at Congaree Swamp is *because* hurricanes have come through on rare occasions. What can you say but that nature works in wonderful and mysterious ways.

LOCATION Congaree Swamp National Monument is located 17 miles southeast of Columbia off SC 48 (Bluff Road). Follow the signs from the turnoff to park entrance and visitor center.

WHEN IT'S OPEN Daily from 8:30 a.m. to 5:00 p.m., except Christmas.

BEST TIMES TO VISIT The colorful fall months are less likely to find Congaree Swamp flooded than are the rainy winter months, and the insect population will be down from the summer. Springtime is also beautiful, as wildflowers bloom and trees leaf out.

WHAT TO DO Hiking, walking the boardwalks, canoeing (bring your own canoe), birdwatching, backcountry camping, fishing, and nature study.

WHERE TO STAY There are numerous hotels and motels in nearby Columbia, the state capital.

FOR MORE INFORMATION Congaree Swamp National Monument, 200 Caroline Sims Road, Hopkins, SC 29061 (803-776-4396).

SOUTH CAROLINA

Four Holes Swamp
(Francis Beidler Forest)

WETLANDS TYPES:

Blackwater cypress-tupelo creek swamp

Cypress-tupelo canopy
Tom Blagden, Jr.

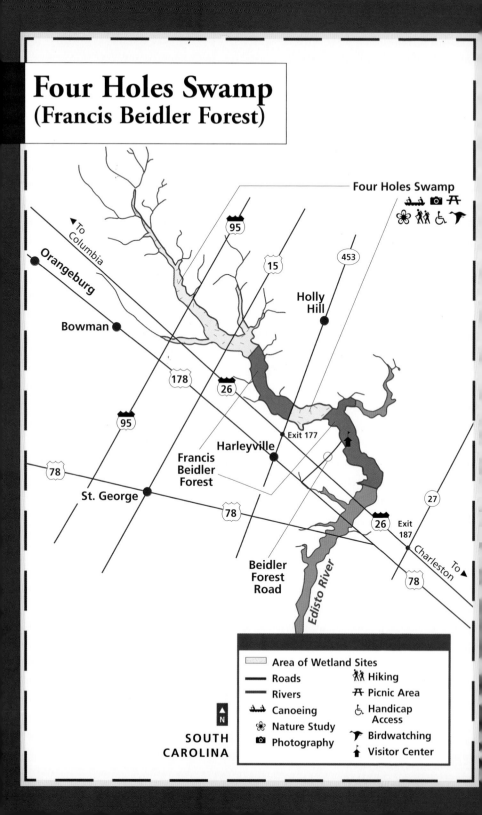

Four Holes Swamp
(Francis Beidler Forest)

Four Holes Swamp

To Columbia

Orangeburg

Bowman

Holly Hill

95

15

453

178

26

95

Harleyville

Francis Beidler Forest

Exit 177

St. George

78

78

26   Exit 187

27

Charleston   To ▲

78

Beidler Forest Road

Edisto River

South Carolina

N

Area of Wetland Sites
Roads
Rivers
Canoeing
Nature Study
Photography

Hiking
Picnic Area
Handicap Access
Birdwatching
Visitor Center

F our Holes Swamp is a "creek swamp," i.e., a self-contained drainage basin that lacks a well-defined main channel, yet through which water courses overground across a broad area. Four Holes snakes its way for 62 miles across the low country through what used to be—and in one exceptional case still is—virgin swamp forest. Eventually, this sluggish creek swamp joins the Edisto River and exits the coast via the ACE Basin (see separate entry). Four Holes Swamp varies in width from one to one-and-a-half miles. Between six and eight creeks (depending on seasonal water levels) meander across it, and in winter and spring, the whole basin is often under water. Nearly 11,000 acres of cypress-gum swamp, mixed hardwood bottomlands, and pine-covered hillocks have been preserved as the Francis Beidler Forest, the awe-inspiring heart of Four Holes Swamp.

Jointly acquired by The Nature Conservancy and the Audubon Society (and managed by the latter), Beidler Forest is one of the premier wetland-interpretation sites in the country. Individuals can take a self-guided walk along an elevated boardwalk, while groups can arrange naturalist-led tours. The boardwalk makes a 1.6-mile loop through the swamp—a cool, well-shaded walk along a corridor that snakes its way among immensely tall trees. Taken at a leisurely pace, with lengthy stops for nature study and quiet reverie, a ramble around the boardwalk will easily occupy half a day. Self-guided tour booklets offer detailed information on plants and wildlife that is keyed to numbered sites along the boardwalk. Guided canoe trips can also be booked in advance for a fee. These excursions allow visitors to paddle up a narrow channel through a land of standing and fallen giants.

Beidler Forest will dash some of the more popular and persistent misconceptions visitors may hold about swamps. For one thing, Four Holes Swamp is not a teeming den of mosquitoes. That is because a current flows here, and mosquitoes prefer to breed in standing water. Second, there is none of the foul, "rotten egg" odor popular lore associates with swamps. To the contrary, the air is clean and even lightly floral-scented. Because of the high level of plant productivity, Four Holes Swamp is a virtual oxygen factory, filtering out pollutants and cleansing the air. Third, it is not infested with poisonous snakes and snapping alligators. Too little sunlight penetrates the canopy to satisfy the alligator's basic need to bask, while the only poisonous snake found in this swamp is the Eastern cottonmouth, which is greatly outnumbered by its non-venomous look-alike, the brown water snake. Fourth,

Overleaf: Autumn leaves and cypress reflections
Tom Blagden, Jr.

this swamp is nothing like the eerie, haunted setting of so much gothic Southern lore. Instead, it is a peaceful, serene, and attractive environment.

So much for all the things the swamp is not. What one will find in the Beidler Forest section of Four Holes Swamp is a vast and varied array of wildlife, including 39 fish species, 40 amphibians, 44 mammals, 50 reptiles, and 140 birds. While none of the flora and fauna are endangered, the habitat that supports this amazing diversity of life forms is itself endangered. Beidler Forest is the largest virgin stand of bald cypress–tupelo gum swamp left in the world. Even so, developmental pressures are creeping toward it from all sides, especially as the city of Charleston (which is only 40 miles away) pushes outward. While the preserve itself will not be overtaken, the effects of encroaching civilization may disturb and pollute Four Holes Swamp. Wildlife that ventures beyond its borders will be adversely impacted.

Some of the more subtle aspects of wetlands ecology can be seen from the boardwalk. Minor elevation changes of only a few feet within a swamp make a great difference in terms of dominant tree species. The lowest-lying areas are constantly inundated, areas that are slightly higher may remain under water several months a year, and still higher areas will be saturated

Prothonotary warbler at nest, by Tom Blagden, Jr.

for even shorter lengths of time. Certain species are favored with adaptations that allow them to live in waterlogged areas that other species find intolerable. That is why bald cypress and tupelo gum grow in standing water while pine trees do not. (Incidentally, the name bald cypress refers to the fact that it is a deciduous needle-leafed conifer, dropping its needles in winter and leaving the bare crown with a bald appearance.)

Both cypress and gum are adapted to swamp life, displaying buttressed bases that flare outward to provide physical stability in a soft substrate. Moreover, cypress trees sprout "knees" at varying distances from the main trunk and have interlocked root systems that ensure further stability. Despite their great height, shallow roots, and watery substrate, the seemingly vulnerable cypress trees at Beidler Forest suffered far less catastrophically during Hurricane Hugo's infamous passage in 1989 than did the pines and hardwoods on upland sites. Only 10 percent of the cypress canopy was lost during the storm, compared with 80 percent of the upland tree canopy. The cypress of Four Holes Swamp owe their survival to the knees, whose height appears to be correlated with water depth. One of the tallest cypress knees you will ever see is a seven-footer that is viewable from the boardwalk at Beidler.

Sometimes these knees assume fanciful and seemingly recognizable shapes. One of the knees by the boardwalk looks like a breaking wave, while another looks like a kneeling Madonna and Child. They serve as homes for prothonotary warblers, the small yellow "swamp canaries" that are among the most common bird species in Four Holes Swamp.

Cypress can live and even thrive outside standing water but are out-competed for such locations by a myriad of other species. Therefore, cypress are largely confined to flooded areas, with only tupelos and water ash for neighbors. Once established, cypress trees can live to great ages, but it takes a rare and precisely timed combination of moisture and drought to launch a cypress seedling. These conditions only occur every hundred years or so, which is why cypress are generally found in even-aged stands. Some of the cypress in Beidler Forest have been cored and dated at more than a thousand years.

The water-tolerant hardwoods that populate the slightly higher flats in the swamp include various oaks, including laurel, overcup, water, and swamp chestnut oak (in order of their tolerance for watery locations, from greater to lesser). Other trees found on the hardwood flats include water hickory, American elm, sweetgum, green ash, and water ash. Loblolly pines colonize the uplands, although many were lost to Hurricane Hugo.

(According to a sanctuary manager, not a day passes that the subject of this "storm of the century" does not come up.) In accordance with the Beidler Forest's guiding philosophy, trees that have fallen, for whatever reason—be it old age or hurricane—are left on the forest floor to decay. That is itself part of a cycle of regeneration, because downed trunks provide habitat for birds and wildlife while also returning nutrients to the soil. In other words, nature knows how to recycle.

Bird life in the forest includes red-shouldered hawks and barred owls, two common swamp denizens that nest in the ferns that grow high in the crowns of old cypress trees. Yellow-bellied sapsuckers peck evenly spaced holes in tree trunks in order to dine on oozing sap and the insects it attracts. Their handiwork is evident on trees beside the boardwalk. Hurricane Hugo had a mixed effect on the bird population. It has benefited birds that prefer scrubby conditions, such as vireos and warblers, while those that live in the canopy have declined in number. All the same, Beidler Forest remains known for its high nesting densities. It is ranked in the top four sites in the country, and it ranks first among all sites east of the Mississippi River.

Mammals move through Four Holes Swamp and are seldom seen. One of the most elusive inhabitants is the bobcat. Though rarely spied by humans, they leave droppings on the boardwalk during the night. Black bear and cougar, alas, have long since been driven from the area. Reptiles and amphibians include box turtles and tree frogs, not to mention a healthy variety of snakes. Lizards dart and scurry up trees and across downed logs.

The farthest point reached by the boardwalk loop is Goodson Lake. The changeable water level of Four Holes Swamp is the subject of a display on the deck overlooking the lake. The primary water sources are springs and storm runoff (mainly the latter). The water level at Four Holes peaks during winter and early spring, dropping steadily through the dry months of summer, and hitting an annual low in early fall before the rains return. The average water depth in Goodson Lake is 4 feet, with an average annual high of 6.9 feet and a low of 2.25 feet. The all-time high was 9.9 feet, reached during Hurricane David in 1979. The record low occurred during the drought of 1986 when lake levels dropped to 1.3 feet. This range is indicative of the extremes that must be tolerated by swamp flora and fauna.

Francis Beidler Forest in Four Holes Swamp is an easy stop for those traveling to or from Charleston. It is a special place—a pure, undefiled world within a larger world in which the natural landscape has been altered beyond recognition. Time spent in Beidler Forest will engender an appreciation for the primeval look of the low country. A walk through this peaceful sanctuary is enough to make a wetlands partisan of even the most unsuspecting visitor.

LOCATION Francis Beidler Forest in Four Holes Swamp is located 40 miles northwest of Charleston. From Charleston, take I-26 west to Exit 187, proceed south on SC 27 to U.S. 78, then follow signs to the sanctuary. From Columbia, or from I-95, take I-26 east to Exit 177, proceed south on SC 453, then east on U.S. 178 through Harleyville, and follow signs to the sanctuary.

WHEN IT'S OPEN Tuesday through Sunday, 9:00 a.m. to 5:00 p.m. Closed Thanksgiving; December 24, 25, 31; and January 1.

BEST TIMES TO VISIT In the spring, when water levels are high and trees are greening and flowering.

WHAT TO DO Walk the boardwalk, canoeing (guided tours only), photography, and nature study.

WHERE TO STAY There are motels and hotels in the town of St. George (I-95 at U.S. 78), 15 miles away, or in Summerville (off I-26, Exit 199). Historic Charleston is only 40 miles from Four Holes Swamp.

FOR MORE INFORMATION Francis Beidler Forest, 336 Sanctuary Road, Harleyville, SC 29448 (803-462-2150).

Reelfoot Lake

WETLANDS TYPES:

Lacustrine, emergent palustrine, cypress swamp

Cypress buttresses and knees skirted with ice on Reelfoot Lake
John Netherton

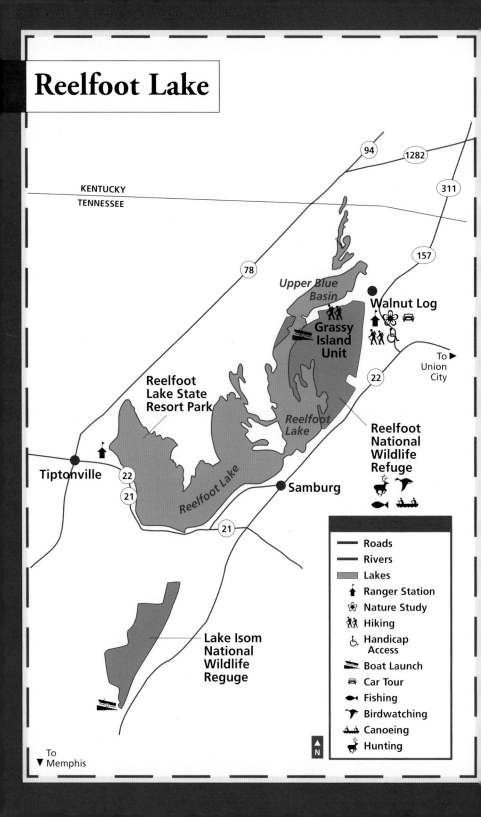

Reelfoot Lake

94 1282

311

KENTUCKY
TENNESSEE

78

157

Upper Blue Basin

Walnut Log

Grassy Island Unit

To Union City

Reelfoot Lake State Resort Park

22

Reelfoot Lake

Reelfoot National Wildlife Refuge

Tiptonville

22

21

Reelfoot Lake

Samburg

21

Lake Isom National Wildlife Reguge

To Memphis

N

Roads
Rivers
Lakes
Ranger Station
Nature Study
Hiking
Handicap Access
Boat Launch
Car Tour
Fishing
Birdwatching
Canoeing
Hunting

hen the subject of earthquakes arises, people think of the West Coast, where massive tectonic plates slowly grind against each other. Seldom are quakes associated with the nation's mid-section, which lies far from any tectonic margins. Yet a series of earthquakes that rank with the most powerful ever recorded in this country occurred in the New Madrid Zone in 1811-12. Straddling the Mississippi River near the junction of Kentucky, Tennessee, Arkansas, and Missouri, a fragmented fault system lies a half-mile underground. The New Madrid earthquakes consisted of 1,874 tremors. Six of them had a magnitude equal to or greater than 7.0 on the Richter scale. Two have been estimated at 8.0, putting them in range of the catastrophic San Francisco earthquake of 1906. The biggest jolt came at 3:00 a.m. on February 7, 1812, visiting cataclysmic changes upon the region's landscape. Yet the New Madrid quakes—named for the epicenter, a Missouri town on the banks of the Mississippi River— resulted in relatively few casualties because the quakes occurred in sparsely populated country.

Anecdotal accounts of the quakes' power read like science fiction. One Missouri town, Little Prairie, virtually disappeared into quicksand. Waterfalls and rapids appeared on the Mississippi River, which reversed itself where the heaving land rose to block its flow, generating an upriver current. Sand-water fountains spewed steam, mud, coal, and carbonized wood. Forests sank and were buried under ten feet of mud and sand. According to an eyewitness account: "The atmosphere was so saturated with sulfurous vapors as to cause total darkness; trees cracked and fell into the roaring Mississippi." The most startling change was the creation of Reelfoot Lake in northwest Tennessee.

One of the main fault segments in the New Madrid Zone runs from Reelfoot Lake across the Mississippi River to the original site of New Madrid, Missouri. This massive lake—actually a series of three contiguous shallow-water basins—was created when forested land in the floodplain of the Mississippi River subsided during the quakes and filled with water. The lake takes its name from a Chickasaw Indian legend that tells of a young Indian chief—named "Reelfoot" because a deformed foot caused him to walk with a reeling motion—who angered the Great Spirit by choosing the beautiful daughter of another tribe as his mate. The Great Spirit stamped his foot in anger, causing the Mississippi River to form a beautiful lake. At the bottom lay Chief Reelfoot, his tribe, and bride. All is now seismologically quiet at Reelfoot Lake. By studying growth rings in ancient cypress trees around the lake, it is believed that quakes such as those of 1811-12 occur at 600-year intervals. That means the ground should not stir for another four centuries. Yet some geologists predict that another mammoth quake will strike the area early in the 21st century.

Reelfoot Lake, 5 miles wide and 14 miles long, is fringed by forests, swamps, and marshes. It is renowned for the many fish species it harbors and the multitude of birds it attracts. Visitors can camp along its shores, take guided sightseeing or fishing trips on its waters, train field glasses on the healthy bald eagle population in the trees and skies above it, and even sleep in comfort at a state park lodge built on pilings that extend over the water.

There are a few rough and rustic trails at Reelfoot Lake State Resort Park and on nearby state and federal wildlife refuges that occupy thousands of acres. Visitors to the 10,428-acre Reelfoot National Wildlife Refuge, for example, can take a 2.5-mile auto tour and a 0.5-mile hiking trail through the bottomland hardwoods and associated wetlands at Grassy Island. They can also explore the Backyard Watchable Wildlife Habitat Showcase, a display of native environments behind the refuge headquarters. One pondside exhibit features common aquatic plants such as arrowhead, primrose-willow, and swamp milkweed.

At Reelfoot Lake State Park, an elevated boardwalk loops among a towering stand of bald cypress at the south end of the lake. With viewing points that face open water, this is the best site on Reelfoot's periphery from which to get a broad, unobstructed view. That is because this mysterious lake, with its odd-shaped basins and extensive swamps and marshes, generally conceals itself. Reelfoot Lake is forested right down to the water's edge. Even then it is sometimes hard to tell where the lake begins because of the emergent plants that blanket its shallow margins. You can only really see the lake from a boat.

For a number of reasons, having mostly to do with siltation resulting from agricultural uses of the land surrounding it, Reelfoot Lake is filling in much more quickly than it would if nature were left to its own devices. Today, the average lake depth is only 5.2 feet. As Reelfoot Lake is steadily invaded from the margins, there is less open water every year—a fact that concerns scientists and outdoorsmen, as well as those who depend on Reelfoot's tourist economy for their livelihood.

Contained within the 153,000-acre Reelfoot Basin are several wetland types: bottomland hardwood forests, tree and shrub swamps, emergent marshes, and open-water wetlands. More than 80 percent of Reelfoot's 24,229 acres of wetlands are classified as open-water wetlands

Giant lotus, by John Netherton

and tree swamps. They account for 9,473 and 10,819 acres, respectively. However, these figures are constantly changing. Emergent marshes are overtaking open water at a precipitous rate. Parts of the lake, particularly on the eastern shores of its basins, are so thick with vegetation—spatterdock (or swampdock), giant lotus, curly pondweed, smartweed, cutgrass, and many others—that they can be crossed only by airboat. In such places, the greenery forms a solid mat and the lake is scarcely a foot deep. Huge, heart-shaped lotus leaves project above the water. A thriving frog population croaks in the shallows. Much of the vegetation is nonpersistent, dying back in winter. During these months, Reelfoot's in-shore areas have more of an open-water look—until the return of spring, which cues even more growth than the year before.

Fish eggs suffocate in the unconsolidated organic muck that accumulates on the lake bottom, dramatically affecting fish populations. The impact of sediment and nutrients washed into the lake from farm fields and eroding loess bluffs in the watershed is severe enough to cause hyper-eutrophication. Sedimentation fills in the lake at a rate of 1.3 inches per year. Some have proposed constructing containment basins along creeks that flow into Reelfoot in order to catch sediment before it reaches the lake. However, this is merely a symptomatic treatment that does not address the larger problem of erosion in the watershed.

Another idea is to draw down the water level between 4 and 8 feet below the normal pool height of 282.2 feet above mean sea level. That height has been maintained with only minor fluctuations since the early 1960s. Lowering it would cause drying out, compaction, and decomposition of lake-bottom sediments. The next step would be flooding the lake four feet above normal pool level to create new spawning grounds. These fluctuations would mimic the seasonal ebb and flow that would otherwise occur if a constant pool height were not maintained by a dam and spillway at Reelfoot's south end.

The extent of the lake's problems can be gauged by this comment from an environmental impact statement prepared in the late 1980s: "Few shorelines are available where the invasion of emergent persistent aquatic vegetation is not readily apparent. Open waters free of emergent nonpersistent or submerged vegetation during the growing season exist only in the deepest parts of the lake." The aging process at Reelfoot Lake has been accelerated due to human influence—mainly agriculture and silviculture—in the watershed. The Army Corps of Engineers estimates that 250,000 tons of sediment, bearing a heavy nutrient load, enters the lake every year. Several inches of sediment accumulates annually in some of the forested bottomlands surrounding the lake. Nutrient inputs from farming activities promote the rapid growth of phytoplankton and aquatic macrophytes, while raising biological oxygen demand to anaerobic levels. Such human-generated inputs are referred to as "cultural eutrophication." In some places, microscopic phytoplankton in the water column is so thick that only one percent of sunlight penetrates one meter below the surface of the lake.

Even though Reelfoot Lake has been stressed by sedimentation and eutrophication, it still offers much in the way of recreation and sights to those who love the outdoors. The lake and its associated wetlands and forests are filled with a varied, extensive inventory of flora and fauna. Here is a sampling:

• *Birds*—Reelfoot Lake is among the most important wintering and stopover areas on the Mississippi flyway. Nearly 250 bird species live here all or part of the year. The varied wetland habitats—open water, shorelines, emergent marshes, and forested wetlands—attract a diversity of bird life. Bald eagles are the most illustrious visitors, reaching a peak population of about 200 during a migratory season that runs from early December through mid-March. Ranger-led eagle-sighting tours are conducted at Reelfoot Lake State Park. If you do not spy an eagle in the wild, three injured ones can be viewed up close at an aviary behind the visitor center. Winter months bring huge flocks of waterfowl to Reelfoot, including

Cypress silhouetted by winter sunset, by John Netherton

400,000 ducks (80 percent of them mallards) and 150,000 geese. During summer, marsh species and wading birds, such as great blue herons and great egrets, are plentiful. (As a side note, large colonies of herons and egrets that once inhabited an area known as Cranetown were permanently scattered in 1957 when dynamite blasts were employed to startle them into flight for dramatic effect in the film *Raintree County.*) When you are in the area, pick up a birdwatcher's checklist at Reelfoot National Wildlife Refuge or Reelfoot Lake State Resort Park.

• *Fish*—It is claimed that Reelfoot Lake is the most productive natural fish hatchery in the nation. More than 70 species have been catalogued in the lake, and 54 are considered permanent inhabitants. Primary game species include bluegill, crappie, catfish, and bass. Such rough fish as carp, shad, bowfin, drum, and gar are also taken. Unfortunately, because of hypereutrophic stresses, rough fish are crowding out the popular game species, and the quality of the lake's fishery is in decline.

• *Reptiles and amphibians*—41 reptile and 28 amphibian species inhabit Reelfoot Lake and environs, including growing numbers of water snakes and frogs, which favor a marsh-swamp habitat. Twelve of Reelfoot's 24 snake species are found in aquatic habitats.

• *Mammals*—Reelfoot Lake's 47 mammal species include such wetland dwellers as raccoon, mink, river otter, muskrat, and beaver. Fox and gray squirrels, raccoons, white-tailed deer, and cottontail and swamp rabbits are abundant game mammals found in Reelfoot's forested bottomlands and uplands.

Reelfoot Lake remains a wondrously vital natural environment, albeit one that is under siege from human activities throughout the watershed. This should be borne in mind as you tour the lake, enjoy all it has to offer, and contemplate its murky, uncertain future.

LOCATION Reelfoot Lake is located in Lake and Obion Counties in northwest Tennessee, approximately 90 miles from Memphis. TN 78 runs along the western side of the lake, while TN 22 runs along the southern and eastern sides. Reelfoot Lake crosses into Kentucky at its north end. The towns of Tiptonville and Samburg are located on the lakeshore. Reelfoot Lake State Resort Park has a visitor center on TN 21/22, just two miles east of Tiptonville, and various recreation areas are scattered around the lake. To get to Reelfoot National Wildlife Refuge, take TN 22 north from Samburg, then follow TN 157 north to refuge headquarters.

WHEN IT'S OPEN Reelfoot Lake State Resort Park is open 8:00 a.m. to 10:00 p.m. (sundown in winter). Reelfoot National Wildlife Refuge is open all year during daylight hours. The visitor center at refuge headquarters is open Monday through Friday, 8:00 a.m. to 4:00 p.m. all year. It is also open on weekends from January through March.

BEST TIMES TO VISIT January for ducks and geese, February for bald eagles, and May for songbirds. Fishing for crappie and bass is good in the fall, while bluegill catches peak in late spring. October is the height of the leaf season.

WHAT TO DO Fishing, birdwatching, hiking, canoeing, and hunting. The Mississippi River is close by, offering extensive recreational opportunities of its own.

WHERE TO STAY The Airpark Inn and Restaurant offers accommodations on Reelfoot Lake. The lodge is part of Reelfoot Lake State Resort Park. Small motels and fish camps are located around the lake and in the towns of Tiptonville and Samburg.

FOR MORE INFORMATION Reelfoot Lake State Resort Park, Route 1, Box 2345, Tiptonville, TN 38079 (901-253-7756); Reelfoot National Wildlife Refuge, 4343 Highway 157, Union City, TN 38261 (901-538-2481).

Wolf River

WETLANDS TYPES:

Bottomland hardwoods, emergent palustrine, gum-cypress swamp

Cardinal flower along the Wolf River
John Netherton

I n states bordering the Mississippi River, where so much of the forested wetlands along its tributaries have been altered or destroyed, the Wolf River is a success story in the making. The headwaters of the Wolf River—which runs from Michigan City, Mississippi, east to Memphis, Tennessee—represent some of the last undisturbed stretches of river habitat in the Mississippi River Valley. Unlike so many creeks and rivers that have been dredged and straightened for flood control or whose floodplains have been logged and cleared for farmland, the upper reaches of the Wolf River in Tennessee have never been channelized. For roughly two-thirds of its total length—from the town of LaGrange to Germantown—the endless meanders that a river naturally carves across a broad floodplain remain intact.

So much prime, forested wetland so close to Memphis makes the Wolf River a prize that has been pursued by developers, agricultural concerns, timber companies, preservationists, and natural resource agencies. The consensus thus far has favored the latter groups, whose members have argued persuasively that the greatest benefits will come from preservation. In its natural state, the Wolf River Greenway provides flood control, soil conservation, water purification, habitat for wildlife, recharge of groundwater aquifers, recreation, and opportunities for environmental education.

Thanks to a grassroots coalition known as the Wolf River Conservancy, large unspoiled tracts in the floodplain of the Wolf River have already been purchased and preserved. Moreover, public awareness has been raised so that even the long-neglected portion of the Wolf that flows through Memphis is considered important enough to save and nurture. Although polluted and abused, the inner city section of the Wolf has a wide greenbelt, and it is not uncommon to see herons, kingfishers, and beaver along the riverbanks. If nurtured, the greenway could be complete from the pristine river corridor upstream right up to the Mississippi, where the Wolf ends its journey.

On any given weekend, canoeists escape the city to negotiate the meandering river, which can be paddled for a dozen incredibly scenic miles between bridge crossings. At one spot, between LaGrange and Moscow, the channel seems to disappear as the current stills and the river disperses across an eerily beautiful gum-cypress swamp. This stretch, known as the Ghost River, has been marked with signs that point the way. It is one of the premier wilderness canoe trails in the East, offering an unforgettable passage beneath an awesome canopy of cypress.

Great blue heron, by John Netherton

On a summer afternoon in 1996, during which the city of Memphis
was experiencing heat in the mid-90s, the swamp forest provided cooling,
bug-free shelter. The temperature by the spring-fed waters of the river, shaded
by hundred-year-old trees, stood in the low 70s. Tying the canoe to a tree
on the riverbank and making a plunge into the river proved more refreshing
still. Such close encounters in this kind of sanctuary, far from the heat of
urbanized clearings and the noise and fumes of highways, give a renewed
appreciation for the beauty of bottomland forests and floodplain swamps.
Their worth extends far beyond the monetary value of the timber that could
be taken in a clearcut.

Wolf River

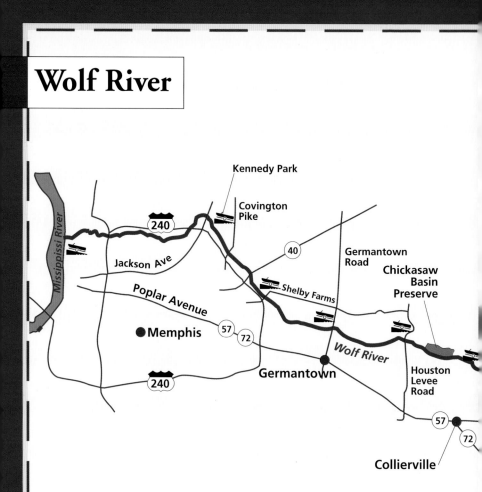

Kennedy Park

Covington Pike

240

40

Germantown Road

Chickasaw Basin Preserve

Jackson Ave

Mississippi River

Poplar Avenue

Shelby Farms

●Memphis

57 72

Wolf River

Germantown

Houston Levee Road

240

57

72

Collierville

N

TENNESSEE

- — Roads
- — Rivers
- Lakes
- Boat Launch
- Canoeing
- Fishing
- Birdwatching
- Photography
- Nature Study

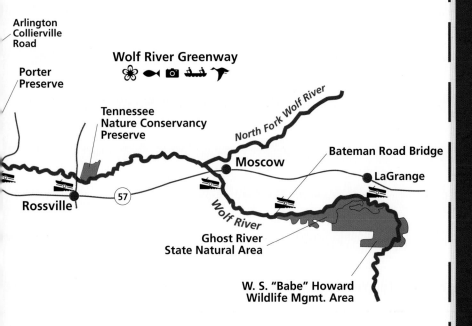

Arlington Collierville Road

Porter Preserve

Wolf River Greenway

Tennessee Nature Conservancy Preserve

North Fork Wolf River

Bateman Road Bridge

Moscow

LaGrange

57

Rossville

Wolf River

Ghost River State Natural Area

W. S. "Babe" Howard Wildlife Mgmt. Area

Such a scenario was narrowly averted at one crucial site on the Wolf River in 1995. During the first half of the decade, the fate of Beasley Farm—a 4,067-acre tract that encompasses the Ghost River swamp— remained uncertain. The story of its purchase and preservation is as absorbing as any "page-turner" penned by Memphis native John Grisham. The parcel had been purchased from the Beasley estate by a land and timber company that planned to auction it off in 69 tracts. Interested bidders included timber companies, hunting clubs, and real estate developers. A consortium of groups—including the Tennessee Wildlife Resources Agency, the Wolf River Conservancy, and the Conservation Fund—struggled to raise the $4 million asking price. The Tennessee Wildlife Resources Agency put up $2.5 million from its wetlands acquisition fund. Intensive efforts to raise the additional $1.5 million targeted other agencies, private corporations, environmental groups, and individuals. With deadlines looming and the gavel about to drop, W. S. "Babe" Howard, a local businessman, stepped in with a pledge of earnest money sufficient to hold off the auction until the outstanding funds could be raised. When the groups could not meet the $4 million figure by yet another pending deadline, Howard himself stepped in to make the purchase and was subsequently reimbursed.

Just what has been preserved thus far? In addition to the Beasley Farm, which now belongs to the state of Tennessee, approximately 600 acres have been donated or purchased. Most recently, a 65-acre tract that includes an area known as Lily Swamp was bought by The Nature Conservancy and added to the inventory of protected lands. The long-range plan is to establish a greenbelt along the Wolf that will run 86 miles, from its headwaters in the state of Mississippi to its mouth at mile 738.6 along the Mississippi River in Memphis, Tennessee. If successful, the Wolf River Greenway would provide flood protection, erosion control, recreation, and much more for rural and urban dwellers alike.

Growing numbers of canoeists already enjoy the upper reaches of the river, particularly between access ramps near the towns of LaGrange and Moscow. Located in Fayette County, this stretch can be divided into two segments. The first segment is between LaGrange and Bateman Road Bridge, east of Moscow. It crosses the Beasley Farm tract, which includes the Ghost River, and is the lengthier (five to six hours) and more challenging canoe trip. Several thriving wetland environments can be viewed along this scenic stretch.

Paddling with the current from east to west, you enter a river that initially meanders in lazy loops across a dense forest of bottomland hardwoods.

Previous page: Expanse of cypress and spatterdock
John Netherton

Smartweed, by John Netherton

The channel disappears entirely as the river dissolves into the vast gum-cypress labyrinth of Ghost River. Without the blue "wilderness canoe trail" signs that have been nailed to trees at short intervals, you might wind up hopelessly lost in these sand-bottomed shallows. On the far side of Ghost River, the channel becomes discernible again, and the big trees give way to bushes, such as Virginia willow, and a more open, lakelike appearance. Eventually the channel deepens and the current picks up speed.

At various times along this route, you have to duck to avoid trees that have fallen across the creek, or paddle around obstructions that include cypress knees and submerged logs. That is in addition to constant turning maneuvers necessary to follow the torturous course charted by the river as it loops upon itself. There is a lesson to be learned here; that is, a stable, healthy river meanders unhurriedly across its floodplain.

Numerous hardwoods, including green ash, red maple, swamp chestnut oak, and blackgum grow on the banks and in the floodplain. The flared, buttressed trunks of bald cypress and tupelo gum are typical of areas inundated much of the year. Indeed, these are the only tree species that can survive for long periods in standing water. Cutgrass grows along the river's edge and, where shallow enough, in the channel itself. Rippling and swaying with the current, cutgrass slows the river by creating turbulence, which causes some of the sediment load to drop out. In areas where the river has a less dis-cernible current, such as Ghost River and the "lake" immediately west of it, spatterdock blankets the surface, especially in summer. This emergent aquatic plant (also known as swampdock or yellow pond-lily) invades open water from the margins during the growing season and dies off in the winter. For this reason, many prefer to canoe the Wolf in cold weather.

More cypress wetlands and easier paddling await in the stretch of the Wolf River that lies between two bridges (Bateman Road and Highway 57) in the vicinity of Moscow. This route makes a wonderful half-day trip, and although it does not include the Ghost River, it is nonetheless scenic and rewarding for novice canoeists or those out for a cool, relaxing afternoon on the river.

The entire LaGrange to Moscow trip, encompassing both segments discussed above, involves about 18 miles of paddling and takes eight to ten hours to complete. One can, in fact, canoe the entire Wolf River all the way to Memphis. A detailed description of canoe trips can be found in a brochure published by the Wolf River Conservancy.

At various times of the year, the Wolf River and its associated wetlands are a riot of colors. These include reds (cardinal flowers), purples (ironweed and swamp iris), yellows (false loosestrife and spatterdock), pinks (swamp rose), blues (blue phlox), and whites (spring cress). Fish live in deep holes throughout the river and swamp. Snakes curl on and under fallen logs. The banded water snake can occasionally be seen shimmying across the water, wriggling a forked tongue. Pyramidal beaver lodges constructed of tree limbs rise above the water here and there.

Mammals that make their home along the river corridor— including sites within the Memphis city limits—include mink and otter. The Wolf River is a haven for 16 varieties of freshwater mussel, including one found nowhere else in Tennessee. Their presence serves as evidence that the Wolf River is a healthy, balanced, and thriving ecosystem. Given the increasing rarity of such environments, the protection and preservation of the Wolf River deserve the highest priority.

LOCATION The Wolf River runs for 86 miles, from Michigan City, Mississippi, to Memphis, Tennessee, where it empties into the Mississippi River. Ten boat ramps and access centers are located along its length. The river passes through Shelby and Fayette Counties in Tennessee. Boat ramps for the segments discussed in the main essay are found beside bridges that cross the Wolf River near the communities of LaGrange and Moscow. For a map of the Wolf River Greenway and a list of canoe trips, contact the Wolf River Conservancy.

WHEN IT'S OPEN Sunrise to sunset.

BEST TIMES TO VISIT The Wolf River is beautiful year round. Spring provides a show of color from flowering plants, summer offers a cooling break from city heat, and fall ushers in striking displays of color. In winter, canoeists will find more open water because of the dieback of nonpersistent vegetation.

WHAT TO DO Canoeing, fishing, birdwatching, photography, and nature study.

WHERE TO STAY Memphis has an abundance of hotels and motels in all price ranges. Motels closer to the headwaters of the Wolf River can be found in or near Collierville.

FOR MORE INFORMATION Wolf River Conservancy, P.O. Box 11031, Memphis, TN 38111-0031 (901-452-6500 or 901-526-9653).

Blanton Forest

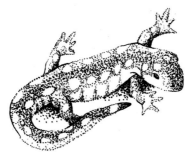

WETLANDS TYPES:

Mountain bogs

Cinnamon ferns in Blanton Forest bogs
John Netherton

Kentucky

I magine stumbling upon a tract of old-growth forest ten times larger than any other stand previously identified in a given state. That is exactly what happened in 1992 to Marc Evans, a botanist for the state of Kentucky. While studying aerial photographs to identify possible natural areas that need protection in the chain of Kentucky State Nature Preserves, Evans noticed that the spreading crowns of trees on Pine Mountain in Harlan County resembled those found in old-growth forests. He traveled to Harlan to investigate and discovered a 2,350-acre tract of old-growth forest composed of mixed mesophytic vegetation, upland oaks, and oak-pine forests that had never been logged. Since the early 1900s the tract had belonged to Grover Blanton, a nature-loving grocer who refused to sell timber rights to his holdings, recognizing the beauty of the woods in their native state. According to his daughters, he "visited his trees every Sunday, like a man to church."

"I'm just amazed that this place exists," Evans marveled in 1992. "How did we miss it? How did we not know?" Having verified its old-growth status, the next step has been acquisition. Obtaining all 2,350 acres of Blanton Forest, plus 4,350 surrounding acres to serve as a buffer, is the task of the Kentucky State Nature Preserves Commission. The state hopes to complete the land acquisition process and open the forest to passive public recreation—birdwatching, photography, and nature study—at some point in the future. Much of the forest and buffer is in private hands, scattered among 90 landowners, which has made for complex and delicate negotiations. A major hurdle was overcome in July 1995 when a 1,075-acre tract, including some of the oldest and most sensitive forest lands, was acquired by the state from two of Blanton's surviving daughters.

When Blanton Forest becomes accessible, visitors will be treated to one of the most diverse and awe-inspiring forests left standing in North America. It is, in fact, the 13th largest stand of old-growth forest in the eastern United States. A canopy of hardwoods—hemlocks, oaks, beeches, maples, and poplars—towers majestically above creeks, bogs, rhododendron thickets, and moist hollows where the air of decomposing organic matter is palpable. Within the depths of the forest, the scene is chaotic and disorderly, just as nature intends. There are trees of all sizes and species, downed timber returning to soil, and dead snags standing beside living 300-year-old giants, their limbs curling in an endless quest for sunlight.

This confused patchwork is actually the way an undisturbed forest is supposed to look. It is a dynamic, species-rich environment in which growth and decay are accelerated and inseparable. Mosses, lichens, ferns, wildflowers,

Eastern mud salamander on sphagnum moss, by John Netherton

and mushrooms grow profusely on the forest floor. The distinctive three-petaled white flowers of trillium join the purples of irises and violets and the pinks and yellows of ladyslippers, creating a riot of colors close to the ground.

From a wetlands perspective, three healthy, undisturbed bogs exist in natural depressions near the top of the mountain. These bogs serve as the headwaters of small creeks that run down the mountain. They harbor rare natural communities and although small are nonetheless important to the forest's biodiversity and to the hydrology of the mountain as a whole. By storing and steadily releasing water, these bogs are critical to the functioning of ecosystems that lie below. The bogs, which have filled with organic material over thousands of years, act like natural sponges. Their spongy nature can be demonstrated by pushing a stick into the muck; it will easily slide a foot or two or so below the surface before resistance is met.

Plant material is slow to decompose in the bogs because of the saturated, waterlogged conditions and relative acidity. In addition to regulating the retention and flow of water down the mountain, the bogs serve to clean and filter water that passes through them. During a daylong hike through Blanton Forest, undertaken after several days of driving rain, our party

Blanton Forest and Pine Mountain Vicinity

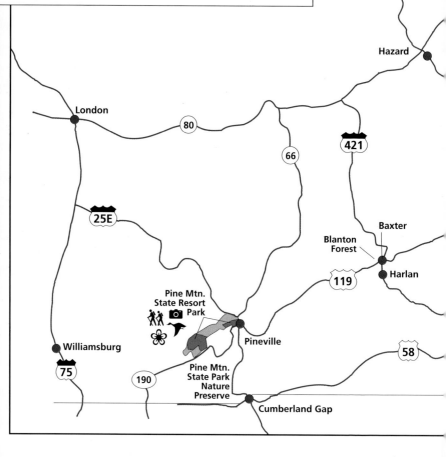

Hazard

London

80

66

421

25E

Baxter

Blanton
Forest

119

Harlan

Pine Mtn.
State Resort
Park

Williamsburg

Pineville

58

75

190

Pine Mtn.
State Park
Nature
Preserve

Cumberland Gap

— Roads
— Rivers
❀ Nature Study
📷 Photography
🚶 Hiking
🦅 Birdwatching
⛺ Camping

N

KENTUCKY

80

Lilley Cornett Woods

15

Whitesburg

KENTUCKY

TENNESSEE

PINE MOUNTAIN

Cumberland River

Pine Mountain State
Park Nature Preserve

Laurel
Cove

Pine Mountain
State Resort Park

190

190

25E

1491

noticed that water entered the lower bogs cloudy and brown but exited clear and clean. Perhaps the best indicator of water quality in the bog-fed streams of Blanton Forest is the presence of the blackside dace, a federally protected minnow that survives only in cold, pure waters.

The three bogs vary in size, shape, orientation, acidity, and in the plant communities they support. The most obvious characteristic of a mountain bog is the absence of tree canopy. These are open, waterlogged depressions dominated by mosses, cinnamon ferns, and a wide variety of other wetland plants. The spongy mosses carpet the floor of the bog, but the cinnamon fern, with its distinctive "fiddleheads"—curled fronds that appear in spring—is the most recognizable bog dweller. Growing in clumps, cinnamon ferns can reach five feet in height. Their origins date back to the Cretaceous period (100 million years ago).

The easternmost bog on Pine Mountain in Blanton Forest is the wettest site and the most likely to have standing water on it at all times of year. Organic material has accumulated to a depth of six feet. Rectangular in shape, it extends for about a hundred yards. Insects, snakes, and amphibians utilize the bog for food, habitat, and reproduction.

The middle bog has an open, meadowlike look, with more wildflowers and fewer cinnamon ferns. A tangle of rhododendron lies along its perimeter. These dense, woody thickets, which line creek banks and moist areas on the mountain, were known as "rhodo hells" by early settlers because of their impassability. The rhododendron's tough, unyielding limbs outline the edge of the second bog, making its open and well-defined area all the more striking.

The westernmost bog is hourglass-shaped, marginally drier, and somewhat less acidic. It supports a smattering of small, stunted trees amid short clumps of cinnamon ferns and a ground cover of sphagnum moss.

Because the peat extends so deeply in these three bogs, they function as superbly effective storage reservoirs. The creeks that run out of them are fed all year long and do not go dry. This is in stark contrast to the flow of water in disturbed, second-growth forests, where creeks tend to run only during the rainy season, quickly discharging the precipitation they receive.

Another intriguing feature found in old-growth forests such as Blanton are pools that are formed in the pits created when dead trees fall over. Not only does this physically till the soil in a forest, but the craters formed by the displaced root mounds also collect water and serve as breeding places for salamanders and frogs. In addition, they provide a source of water for wildlife. When a large old tree topples, space opens up in the canopy for

Previous page: Morning mist over Cumberland Mountains
John Netherton

younger trees, the fallen trunk serves as habitat for ground dwellers, and its decomposition returns nutrients and organic matter to the soil in the ultimate act of recycling. The alterations brought to the landscape by naturally falling trees is known as pit-and-mound topography.

There is even more of interest here, particularly from a geological perspective. The little creeks that rush down the mountain occasionally disappear under ground, only to resurface some distance farther downslope. Another unusual feature is a vast, sloping field of pitted, textured rock that overlooks Harlan County and the Cumberland Mountains from an elevation of 2,000 feet. Black snakes sun themselves on the rocks, dropping over the sides onto the tree limbs below when humans approach.

Blanton Forest lies along Pine Mountain, a ridgetop mountain that runs across three states (Kentucky, Virginia, and Tennessee) for 120 miles. The only break in the ridge is at Pineville, where the Cumberland River flows through a gap in the mountains.

Few mountain bogs and old-growth forests have survived the crosscut saw and the press of civilization. Prior to the discovery of Blanton Forest, scientists believed that only about 1,000 acres of old-growth forest remained in all of Kentucky. Now that number has tripled, and we should all be very grateful indeed for the preservationist instinct of Blanton Forest's visionary namesake and former owner.

LOCATION Blanton Forest is located on the south slope of Pine Mountain in Harlan County, Kentucky.

WHEN IT'S OPEN Blanton Forest is not yet open to the public; however, plans are under way to allow access for passive recreation by the year 2001. Other opportunities for visiting old-growth forests are available in two additional locations in the Pine Mountain vicinity, including Pine Mountain State Resort Park and State Nature Preserve, and Lilley Cornett Woods (see map). Public access to Lilley Cornett Woods is by guided tours on designated trails; Pine Mountain State Resort Park has hiking trails and numerous other facilities. The resort park is open year round, except for a week at Christmas.

WHERE TO STAY There are motels in Harlan and a lodge, cottages, and campsites in the state park.

FOR MORE INFORMATION Kentucky State Nature Preserves Commission, 801 Schenkel Lane, Frankfort, KY 40601 (502-573-2886); Lilley Cornett Woods, HC 63, Box 2710, Skyline, KY 41851 (606-633-5828). Pine Mountain State Resort Park, 1050 State Park Road, Pineville, KY 40977 (606-337-3066).

Cave Run Lake

WETLANDS TYPES:

Restored and created palustrine wetlands, ridgetop wetlands

Foxtail grass and cattails around Cave Run Lake
John Netherton

N umerous wetlands lie in the floodplains of the small creeks that flow through the Daniel Boone National Forest near Cave Run Lake in eastern Kentucky. These shallow, emergent marshes teem with life. Their margins are choked with freshwater aquatic plants, including cattail, arrowhead, sedges, bulrush, and smartweed. They are surrounded by acres of grass and clover. This network of marshes and fields provides food and habitat for Canada geese, ducks, and other native and migratory waterfowl—222 bird species in all, according to recent counts. Frogs, toads, and snakes inhabit the fields and shallows. On a warm afternoon in early May, a pair of hooded mergansers could be seen scooting across a pond. Turkey vultures dried themselves on distant perches high in the bare limbs of snags. Canada geese patrolled a field, warning away human visitors while their goslings foraged.

The honking of geese, flapping of wings, croaking of frogs, watery plopping of turtles, and endless buzzing of insects attest to the vibrant dynamism of these marshes. Thick stands of cattail and marsh grasses provide a formidable border on their fringes. The only thing more remarkable than the abundance of life forms found on the 168 acres of emergent palustrine wetlands adjoining Beaver, Scott, and Brushy Creeks near Cave Run Lake is the fact that these wetlands did not even exist until a few years ago.

It is a testament both to natural resiliency and human enterprise that these wetlands have become thriving magnets for wildlife and aquatic plants in a short period of time. Although 81 percent of the wetlands that existed in Kentucky at the time of its settlement by Europeans have been eliminated—making it the seventh most wetlands-depleted state in the United States—pioneering restoration projects like those undertaken at Cave Run Lake are gradually restoring ecological associations that existed before so many of the state's marshy bottomland areas were drained, logged, and converted to farmland. Those who live near or visit Cave Run Lake now enjoy and appreciate the wetlands that have suddenly reappeared on the landscape.

Those uses and functions include serving as a natural means of flood control by accommodating overflow from adjoining creeks during storms and times of peak precipitation; as habitats that harbor unique associations of species; as filters that clean and purify the water that passes through them; and as breeding and feeding grounds for an amazing diversity of bird life. Surveys have determined that nearly 90 percent of all ducks and geese in eastern Kentucky use the existing, restored, and created wetlands at Cave

Lone waterfowl at sunset, by John Netherton

Run Lake. Until restoration projects were undertaken, Canada geese and hooded mergansers were rarely seen in eastern Kentucky in modern times.

Credit for this wetlands renaissance goes to Tom Biebighauser, a U.S. Forest Service wildlife biologist who orchestrated the creation of wetlands at Cave Run Lake. He freely admits that he came to the project with no training in wetlands restoration. Using an approach that ought to give hope to anyone interested in wetlands restoration, he simply learned by doing and by consulting experts in the field, locals with mechanical know-how and memories of the way things were, and historical records that confirmed the existence of wetlands along these creeks and streams. As leased parcels of unproductive, low-lying farmland along the creeks were taken out of production and returned to the Forest Service, Biebighauser thought: "Why can't I restore a wetland instead of returning it to tillable land?"

Because no historical accounts precisely describe the location and plant makeup of wetlands that existed in prior centuries, some of the recently placed wetlands may technically be "created," as opposed to "restored." However, nature has adapted to them just fine. Long-dormant seeds and spores buried in the ground, along with those carried on the legs and wings of migratory birds, have given rise to prospering aquatic plant communities.

Documentary evidence of wetlands does exist in the surviving memoirs of local settlers of the 1700s who noted the presence of beaver dams and Canada geese. There are also detailed notations by a botanist, Clarendon Peck, who catalogued plant species along the Licking River.

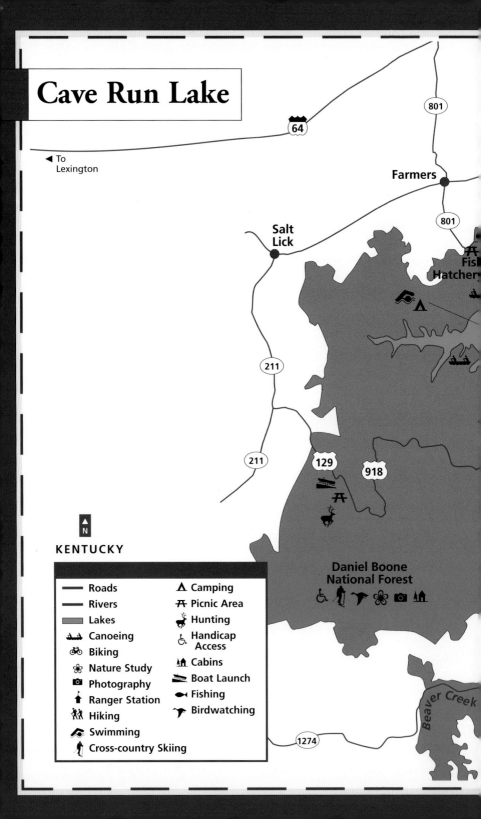

Cave Run Lake

64

◄ To
Lexington

801

Farmers

801

**Salt
Lick**

**Fish
Hatchery**

211

211

129

918

**Daniel Boone
National Forest**

N

KENTUCKY

—	Roads	▲	Camping
—	Rivers	禾	Picnic Area
▭	Lakes	🦌	Hunting
Canoeing		Handicap Access
🚲	Biking	Cabins
✿	Nature Study	Boat Launch
📷	Photography	Fishing
♦	Ranger Station	Birdwatching
🚶	Hiking	
🏊	Swimming	
🎿	Cross-country Skiing	

Beaver Creek

1274

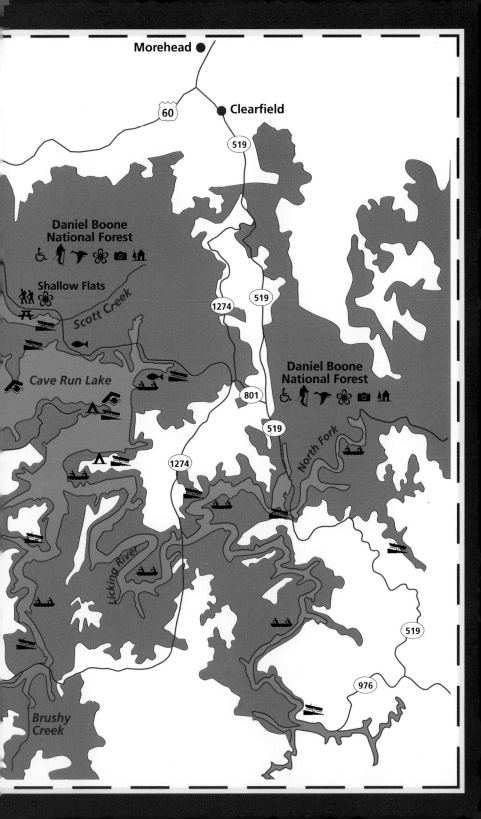

(Its damming by the Army Corps of Engineers created Cave Run Lake in the mid-1960s.) Peck's botanical inventory was used by Biebighauser in his initial plantings. Further recollections were provided by a local individual who originally helped drain many of the fields for farming and now finds himself hired to do the same task in reverse.

The process of creating a shallow, freshwater wetland that successfully mimics the beaver ponds and floodplain sloughs originally found along the creeks involves scraping the topsoil to one side, digging a depression, constructing a levee to retain water, replacing the thin layer of topsoil in the depression, and then emplacing a control structure to allow the water level to be raised or lowered. At first, these depressions look like farm ponds, but they quickly fill in with aquatic vegetation and become wetlands. Raising or lowering the water level in a seasonal mimicry of nature enhances their function and appearance as native wetlands.

To date, 116 wetlands—each averaging 1.5 acres—have been established along creeks surrounding Cave Run Lake. Formally known as the Wild Wings Challenge Cost-Share Project, the effort was conceived by Biebighauser in 1991 as a way to restore and establish wetlands for waterfowl, wading birds, shorebirds, and Canada geese. The lack of shallow-water habitat had been the main limiting factor in attracting and maintaining waterfowl populations in eastern Kentucky. Seasonal fluctuations in water level by the Corps of Engineers at Cave Run Lake only exacerbated that situation. That is to say, the principal reasons for creating the lake—flood control and recreation—necessitated high lake levels in summer (for recreation) and low ones in winter (to leave room for spring runoff). Aquatic plants are not able to survive low water levels in the winter. The wetlands around Cave Run Lake are managed so that they fill with water by winter. Plants submerged in the wetlands provide abundant food for waterfowl.

Balancing nesting season demands against those of migration is part of the challenge that the Forest Service calls "moist soil management." By providing food, habitat, and nesting areas for waterfowl, the created wetlands and associated fields—planted in grass, clover, wheat, and corn— redress these imbalances at Cave Run Lake. Wood duck boxes and tubs for nesting geese have been placed in and around the wetlands. The project has succeeded so well that in 1993 it won the U.S. Forest Service's "Taking

Previous page: Emergent freshwater marsh along the lake's margin
John Netherton

Spotted jewelweed, by John Netherton

Wing" award, which recognizes efforts in protecting and improving wetlands on forest lands.

Wild Wings is a cooperative partnership involving organizations and individuals, including Ducks Unlimited, the Kentucky Department of Fish and Wildlife Resources, the Rowan County Wildlife Club, the Menifee County Fish and Game Club, the Bath County Future Farmers of America, and scientists and students at Morehead State University. Over 300 people, including students from abroad and adults and teenagers from all over eastern Kentucky, have logged more than 2,500 volunteer days on the Wild Wings project.

One enterprising young man, Paul Kornman, has been instrumental in bringing a created wetland to life. This ambitious teenager planned and oversaw construction of a gravel-surfaced loop nature trail and planted a shallow pond in native vegetation, hastening its reversion to wetlands. He conducted an inventory of nearby sites, identifying 44 species native to eastern Kentucky wetlands. Then he transplanted specimens of each to his new location. His list included such common freshwater marsh dwellers as smartweed, spatterdock (or swampdock), cattail, buttonbush, and arrowhead. For his work, Kornman received Eagle Scout certification.

Meanwhile, Tom Biebighauser continues to press ahead with more wetlands projects. In addition to restored and created wetlands around Cave Run Lake and its creeks, he has created numerous small pools and ridgetop wetlands. The pools mimic those scoured by eddies that form when trees fall across moving water, and they serve as spawning grounds for salamanders and other amphibians. His ridgetop wetlands imitate the pit-and-mound depressions found in old-growth forests when fallen trees leave pits (where they have been uprooted) and mounds (where the roots and soil now lie above the ground). The pits fill with water, serving as breeding areas while storing water that is used by ridge-dwelling species. Biebighauser proudly notes that the first site on the whole of the Cumberland Plateau in which a federally protected Indiana bat was found reproducing was over the manmade ridgetop wetlands at Cave Run Lake.

Perhaps the greatest success story to date is that of the Canada goose population. Four acres of wetlands and six acres of grassy meadows were created on the shores of Cave Run Lake at Shallow Flats. Back in 1978, an initial population of 33 free-flying giant Canada geese was released here. Reshaping the attitudes of locals from capturing to protecting these newcomers was important in reestablishing a breeding population at Cave Run Lake. In addition to creating wetlands and cultivating adjacent fields in grass and clover, more than 350 nesting structures have been constructed. Each June, the geese are counted and banded. From the initial population of 33 in 1978, the flock grew to a healthy 2,000 geese by 1995. Visitors to Cave Run Lake can observe giant Canada geese all year at the Shallow Flats wildlife viewing area. Although they may not realize it, they will also be looking out on one of the most successful wetlands restoration projects in the country.

LOCATION Cave Run Lake is located near Morehead, Kentucky, in the Daniel Boone National Forest. For maps and orientation, visit the Morehead Ranger Station and Visitor Center. To get there from Morehead, take I-64 west to the KY 801 Exit, then proceed south to the visitor center.

WHEN IT'S OPEN The visitor center is open daily from 8:00 a.m. to 5:00 p.m. between Memorial Day and Labor Day and from 8:30 a.m. to 4:00 p.m. on weekdays the rest of the year (except for federal holidays).

BEST TIMES TO VISIT Canada geese are captured and banded the third week of June each year. Summer is an opportune time for activities on Cave Run Lake. Cooler weather brings fall colors to the oaks and maples of the surrounding forest. Migrating ducks and geese begin arriving in late fall and early winter.

WHAT TO DO Boating, camping, picnicking, swimming, fishing, hiking, cross-country skiing, birdwatching, hunting, photography, and nature study.

WHERE TO STAY There are primitive and developed campgrounds at Cave Run Lake. In addition, motels and hotels are located off I-64, especially in nearby Morehead.

FOR MORE INFORMATION Morehead Ranger District, 2375 KY 801 South, Morehead, KY 40351 (606-784-6428).

Additional Wetland Sites

Following is information on additional wetland sites suitable for outdoor recreation and environmental education:

GEORGIA

Eufaula National Wildlife Refuge—Straddling the Georgia and Alabama border, the sloughs, savannas, forests, and fields of Eufaula National Wildlife Refuge attract great numbers and varieties of birds, including prothonotary warblers, wood storks, bald eagles, and peregrine falcons. Located beside Lake George, a manmade reservoir on the Chatahoochee River, the refuge also provides habitat for alligator, beaver, otter, deer, and bobcat. Bring a canoe for best viewing of birds and wildlife. Contact Eufaula National Wildlife Refuge, Route 2, Box 97B, Eufaula, AL 36027 (205-687-4065).

Magnolia Springs State Park—The springs at this state park produce about nine million gallons of water each day. Lacustrine wetlands, a cypress-gum swamp, and a shrub-bay pocosin/longleaf-pine savanna can be found at this 948-acre park. The grounds include a campground, two nature trails, a fishing dock, observation deck, and canoe rental station. While in the area, visit the Millen National Fish Hatchery and Aquarium. Contact Magnolia Springs State Park, Route 5, Box 488, Millen, GA 30442 (912-982-1660).

Ocmulgee River—Located in the Oconee National Forest in north central Georgia, the Ocmulgee River Trail passes through a forest of mixed pines and bottomland hardwoods in the river's floodplain. The three-mile trail follows the river so closely that it is subject to flooding at certain times of the year. The rewards of this proximity include the possibility of sighting such river dwellers as mink, beaver, muskrat, and turtles. Spring wildflowers bloom on the hillsides above the floodplain. There are other trails in the area, as well as camping, fishing, and hunting. Contact U.S. Forest Service, Oconee Ranger District, 349 Forsyth Street, Monticello, GA 31064 (404-468-2244).

Sapelo Island—This pristine barrier island is the fourth largest in Georgia. Sapelo has been designated a Natural Estuarine Research Reserve and is the site of the University of Georgia's Marine Institute. The island consists of beaches and dunes, maritime forest, and an extensive network of salt marshes. Remains of human settlements dating back 4,000 years have been found at archaeological sites on the island. Interpretive tours of the island are offered to school groups and the general public. Contact Sapelo Island NERR, Georgia Department of Natural Resources, Sapelo Island, GA 31327 (912-485-2251).

KENTUCKY

Metropolis Lake—Way out in western Kentucky lies a lake and swamp in the floodplain of the Ohio River. Metropolis Lake, located west of Paducah at the end of KY 996, faces the town of Metropolis, which lies directly across the river in Illinois. Stands of bald cypress and swamp tupelo contribute to the stateliness of this remote setting, which looks the way floodplains of great rivers used to look before they were drained and cleared. Contact the Kentucky State Nature Preserves Commission, 801 Schenkel Lane, Frankfort, KY 40801 (502-573-2886).

NORTH CAROLINA

Cedar Island—Bordered by Core and Pamlico Sounds, Cedar Island possesses one of the largest and least spoiled salt marshes on the East Coast. It is a haven for black ducks and migratory waterfowl. It is an especially good place to observe the effects of irregular tidal flooding and salinity upon plant zonation. Contact Cedar Island National Wildlife Refuge, Route 12, Cedar Island, NC (919-225-2511).

Croatan National Forest—Wetlands common to the outer Coastal Plain of North Carolina—including pocosins, savannas, and wet flats—can be found in this 157,000-acre national forest in the southeast corner of the state. Croatan is a longleaf- and loblolly-pine forest whose peat swamps harbor carnivorous plants and whose marshes, creeks, and bays attract migratory waterfowl. Be sure to visit Great Lake and Catfish Lake Pocosins. Contact Croatan National Forest, 435 Thurman Road, New Bern, NC 28560 (919-638-5628).

Goose Creek State Park—At the point where Goose Creek meets the Pamlico River east of Washington is an area of brackish marshes, swamp forests, and shrub thickets. The marshes contain stands of sawgrass and black needlerush that reach eight feet in height. A system of boardwalk trails through the park offers excellent access to the different wetlands environments. Contact Goose Creek State Park, Route 2, P.O. Box 372, Washington, NC 27889 (919-923-2291).

Roanoke River Bottomlands—For 20 miles along U.S. 17/13 north of Williamston, dense stands of bottomland hardwoods and swamp forest line the floodplain of the Roanoke River, harboring a rich assortment of wildlife such as bobcats and black bears. The area includes 21,000 acres of mature cypress and tupelo gum forest. The brownwater ecosystem of the lower Roanoke has been deemed one of the "last great places" by The Nature Conservancy. Contact Roanoke River National Wildlife Refuge, Bertie County Courthouse, Windsor, NC 27983 (919-794-5326).

SOUTH CAROLINA

Aiken State Park—Located in the "lower midlands" of South Carolina, near the Georgia state line, Aiken State Park lies along the South Edisto River. The area includes a blackwater river swamp (penetrated by the Edisto River Canoe Trail), four spring-fed lakes, and dry sandhills. The aptly named Jungle Trail is thickly bordered with switchcane, various bays and ferns, sweet pepperbush, and wax myrtle. Contact Aiken State Park, 1125 State Park Road, Windsor, SC 29856 (803-649-2857).

Cape Romain—This 60,000-acre island refuge northeast of Charleston encompasses sandy beaches and upland oak forests, as well as salt, brackish, and freshwater marshes. Cape Romain attracts oystercatchers, terns, egrets, and herons in profusion. Loggerhead turtles lay more eggs on its beaches than at any other site on the South Carolina coast. Access is by boat only, with a concessionaire making regular trips to Bull's Island (largest of the refuge's 17 islands). Contact Cape Romain National Wildlife Refuge, 390 Bull's Island Road, Awendaw, SC 29429 (803-928-3368).

Woods Bay State Park—Woods Bay is a Carolina bay wetland located on the Coastal Plain. A boardwalk and a canoe trail provide access into the interior of this swampy depression. Habitats range from open savanna at the bay's east end to cypress swamp elsewhere. Contact Woods Bay State Park, Route 1, Box 208, Olanta, SC 29114 (803-659-4445).

TENNESSEE

Hatchie National Wildlife Refuge—Like the Wolf River (see text entry), the Hatchie River is one of the last unchannelized rivers in the lower Mississippi River Valley. It courses along in lazy meanders, creating oxbow lakes and sloughs. The sort of species diversity that is typically found in rich bottomlands—80 percent of which have vanished in the lower Mississippi Valley due to clearing—is very much in evidence in the Hatchie's oak-hickory forests and cypress-gum swamps. More than 200 bird species have been catalogued on these timbered lowlands, including rare Swainson's warblers and large populations of wintering and migratory waterfowl. Contact Hatchie National Wildlife Refuge, P.O. Box 187, Brownsville, TN 38012 (901-772-0501).

For general, educational, technical, and regulatory information on wetlands, call the EPA Wetlands Information Hotline at 1-800-832-7828.

Flora and Fauna
Trees, Shrubs, and Plants

Alabama Milkvine (*Matelea alabamaensis*)
American Beech (*Fagus grandifolia*)
American Elm (*Ulmus americana*)
American Holly (*Ilex opaca*)
American Sycamore (*Platanus occidentalis*)
Arrowhead (*Sagittaria latifolia*)
Arrowwood (*Viburnum* sp.)
Atamasco Lily (*Zephyranthes atamasca*)
Atlantic White Cedar
 (*Chamaecyparis thyoides*)
Bald cypress/Cypress (*Taxodium distichum*)
Beech/American Beech (*Fagus grandifolia*)
Bitternut Hickory (*Carya cordiformis*)
Black Needlerush (*Juncus roemerianus*)
Blackgum (*Nyssa sylvatica*)
Bladderwort (*Utricularia* sp.)
Blueberry (*Vaccinium* sp.)
Blue Phlox (*Phlox* sp.)
Bulrush (*Scirpus* sp.)
Buttonbush (*Cephalanthus occidentalis*)
Cabbage Palmetto (*Sabal palmetto*)
Cardinal Flower (*Lobelia cardinalis*)
Cattail (*Typha* sp.)
Cedars (*Chamaecyparis thyoides*)
Cinnamon Fern (*Osmunda cinnamomea*)
Clover (*Trifolium* sp.)
Cordgrass/Smooth Cordgrass
 (*Spartina alterniflora*)
Curly Pondweed (*Potamogeton crispus*)
Cutgrass (*Leersia* sp.)
Dogwood (*Cornus florida*)
Duckweed (*Lemna* sp.)
Eastern Hemlock (*Tsuga canadensis*)
False Loosestrife (*Lysimachia* sp.)
Ferns (Pteridophytes)
Fetterbush (*Leucothoe racemosa*)
Foxtail Grass (*Alopecurus* sp.)
Franklinia (*Gordonia altamaha*)
Gallberry (*Ilex glabra*)
Georgia plume (*Elliottia racemosa*)
Glasswort (*Salicornia* sp.)
Grass Pink (*Calopogon pulchellus*)

Green Ash (*Fraxinus pennsylvanica*)
Greenbrier (*Smilax* sp.)
Hairy Rattleweed (*Bapitista arachnifera*)
Hawthorn (*Crataegus* sp.)
Hickories (*Carya* sp.)
Irises (*Iris* sp.)
Ironweed (*Vernonia* sp.)
Ironwood (*Carpinus caroliniana*)
Jewelweed/Spotted Touch-Me-Not/
 Pale Touch-Me-Not (*Impatiens capensis*)
Joe-Pye-Weed (*Eupatorium* sp.)
Ladyslippers (*Cypripedium* sp.)
Laurel Oak (*Quercus laurifolia*)
Live Oak (*Quercus virginiana*)
Loblolly Bay (*Gordonia lasianthus*)
Loblolly Pine (*Pinus taeda*)
Longleaf Pine (*Pinus palustris*)
Lotus (*Nelumbo lutea*)
Magnolia (*Magnolia* sp.)
Maples (*Acer* sp.)
Mockernut Hickory (*Carya tomentosa*)
Mountain Laurel (*Kalmia latifolia*)
Oak (*Quercus* sp.)
Overcup Oak (*Quercus lyrata*)
Palmetto (*Sabal minor*)
Pawpaw (*Asimina* sp.)
Pine (*Pinus* sp.)
Pitcher-Plant (*Sarracenia* sp.)
Poison Ivy (*Toxicodendron radicans*)
Poison Sumac (*Toxicodendron vernix*)
Pond Cypress (*Taxodium ascendens*)
Pond Pine (*Pinus serotina*)
Primrose-Willow (*Ludwigia decurrens*)
Radford's Balm/Radford's Dicerandra
 (*Dicerandra radfordiana*)
Redbay (*Persea palustris*)
Red Maple (*Acer rubrum*)
Redhead Grass (*Panicum* sp.)
Reedgrass (*Phragmites* sp.)
Resurrection Fern (*Polypodium polypodioides*)
Rhododendron (*Rhododendron* sp.)
River Birch (*Betula nigra*)

Trees, Shrubs, Plants *continued*

Rosebud Orchid (*Cleistes divaricata*)
Royal Fern (*Osmunda regalis*)
Sedges (Cyperaceae)
Shumard Oak (*Quercus shumardii*)
Slash Pine (*Pinus elliottii*)
Smartweed (*Polygonum* sp.)
Soft Rush (*Juncus effusus*)
Sourwood (*Oxydendrum arboreum*)
Southern Red Oak/Swamp Red Oak
   (*Quercus falcata*)
Spanish Moss (*Tillandsia usneoides*)
Spatterdock/Swampdock
   (*Rumex verticillatus*)
Sphagnum Moss (*Sphagnum* sp.)
Speckled Alder (*Alnus incana*)
Spikegrass (*Distichlis spicata*)
Spring Cress (*Cardamine bulbosa*)
Sundew (*Drosera* sp.)
Swamp Chestnut Oak (*Quercus michauxii*)
Swamp Iris (*Iris* sp.)
Swamp Loosestrife (*Decodon verticillatus*)
Swamp Milkweed (*Asclepias incarnata*)
Swamp Rose (*Rosa palustris*)
Swampbay (*Persea palustris*)
Sweet Pepperbush (*Clethra alnifolia*)
Sweet Pitcher-Plant (*Sarracenia rubra*)
Sweetbay (*Magnolia virginiana*)
Sweetgum (*Liquidambar styraciflua*)
Switchcane (*Arundinaria gigantea*)
Tickseed (*Coreopsis* sp.)

Titi/Swamp Cyrilla (*Cyrilla racemiflora*)
Toothache Grass (*Ctenium aromaticum*)
Trailing Arbutus (*Epigaea repens*)
Trillium (*Trillium* sp.)
Trumpet-Leaf Pitcher-Plant (*Sarracenia flava*)
Tulip Poplar (*Liriodendron tulipifera*)
Tupelo Gum (*Nyssa sylvatica* var. *biflora*)
Turkey Oak (*Quercus laevis*)
Venus Flytrap (*Dionaea muscipula*)
Violets (*Viola* sp.)
Virginia Willow (*Itea virginica*)
Water Ash (*Fraxinus caroliniana*)
Water Lily (*Nymphaea odorata*)
Water Oak (*Quercus nigra*)
Water Tupelo/Tupelo Gum (*Nyssa aquatica*)
Waterweed (*Elodea* sp.)
Wax Myrtle (*Myrica cerifera*)
White Cedar (*Chamaecyparis thyoides*)
White Oak (*Quercus alba*)
White Pine (*Pinus strobus*)
White-Topped Sedge (*Dichromena colorata*)
Wigeongrass/Ditchgrass (*Ruppia maritima*)
Wild Celery (*Angelica lucida*)
Willow Oak (*Quercus phellos*)
Wiregrass (*Aristida stricta*)
Yellow Pond-Lily (*Nuphar luteum*)
Yellow Poplar/Tulip Tree
   (*Liriodendron tulipifera*)
Yellow Root (*Xanthorhiza simplicissima*)
Zenobia (*Zenobia pulverulenta*)

Mammals

Beaver (*Castor canadensis*)
Black Bear (*Ursus americanus*)
Bobcat (*Felis rufus*)
Cottontail Rabbit (*Sylvilagus floridanus*)
Fox Squirrel (*Sciurus niger*)
Gray Squirrel (*Sciurus carolinensis*)
Ground Squirrel (*Tamias striata*)
Indiana Bat (*Chiroptera*)
Mink (*Mustela vison*)

Muskrat (*Ondatra zibethicus*)
Opposum (*Didelphis virginiana*)
Raccoon (*Procyon lotor*)
Red Fox (*Vulpes vulpes*)
River Otter (*Lutra canadensis*)
Southern Black Bear (*Ursus arctos*)
Swamp Rabbit (*Sylvilagus aquaticus*)
White-Tailed Deer (*Odocoileus virginianus*)

Birds

Anhinga (*Anhinga anhinga*)
Bald Eagle (*Haliaeetus leucocephalus*)
Barred Owl (*Strix varia*)
Black Skimmer (*Rynchops niger*)
Canada Goose (*Branta canadensis*)
Canvasback (*Aythya valisineria*)
Coot (*Fulica americana*)
Eastern Wood Pewee (*Contopus virens*)
Egret (*Casmerodius albus egretta*)
Florida Sandhill Crane
  (*Grus canadensis pratensis*)
Glossy Ibis (*Plegadis falcinellus*)
Great Blue Heron (*Ardea herodias*)
Greater Sandhill Crane (*Grus canadensis*)
Green Heron (*Butorides striatus*)
Hooded Merganser (*Lophodytes cucullatus*)
Indigo Bunting (*Passerina cyanea*)
Kentucky Warbler (*Oporornis formosus*)
Kingfisher (*Megacercyle alcyon*)
Lousiana Waterthrush (*Seiurus motacilla*)
Mallard Duck (*Anas platyrhynchos*)
Mourning Dove (*Zenaidura macroura*)

Osprey (*Pandion haliaetus*)
Pintail Duck (*Anas acuta tzitzihoa*)
Prothonotary Warbler (*Protonotaria citrea*)
Quail/Bobwhite (*Colinus virgianus*)
Red-Cockaded Woodpecker
  (*Dendrocopus borealis*)
Red-Shouldered Hawk (*Buteo lineatus*)
Royal Tern (*Sterna maxima*)
Sandpiper (Scolopacidae)
Snipe (*Capella gallinago*)
Snow Goose (*Chen hyperborea*)
Swainson's Warbler (*Limnothlypis swainsonii*)
Tundra Swan/Whistling Swan
  (*Cygnus columbianus*)
Turkey (*Meleagris gallopavo*)
Turkey Vulture (*Cathartes aura*)
Vireo (*Vireonidae* sp.)
White Ibis (*Plegadis chihi*)
Wood Duck (*Aix sponsa*)
Wood Stork (*Mycteria americana*)
Woodpecker (Picidae)
Yellow-Bellied Sapsucker (*Sphyrapicus varius*)

Fish

Black Crappie (*Pomoxis nigramaculatus*)
Blackside Dace (*Phoxinus cumverlandensis*)
Bluegill (*Lepomis macrochirus*)
Bowfin (*Amia calva*)
Carp (*Cyprinus carpio*)
Catfish (Ictaluridae)
Chain Pickerel (*Esox niger*)

Drum (*Aplodinotus grunniens*)
Gar (Lepisosteidae)
Herring (Clupeidae)
Largemouth Bass (*Micropterus salmoides*)
Shad (*Alosa sapidissima*)
Sunfish (Centrarchidae)
Trout (Salmonidae)

Amphibians and Reptiles

American Alligator (*Alligator mississippiensis*)
Banded Water Snake (*Nerodia fasciata*)
Bird-Voiced Tree Frog (*Hyla avivoca*)
Box Turtle (*Terrapene carolina*)
Brown Water Snake (*Nerodia taxispilota*)
Bullfrog (*Rana catesbeiana*)
Carolina Gopher Frog (*Rana capito*)
Chorus Frog (*Pseudacris* sp.)
Cooter/Pond Turtle (*Chrysemys concinna*)
Eastern Cottonmouth
  (*Agkistrodon piscivorus*)
Eastern Diamondback Rattlesnake
  (*Crotalus adamanteus*)
Eastern Mud Salamander
  (*Pseudotriton montanus*)

Frog (Ranidae)
Gopher Tortoise (*Gopherus polyphemus*)
Green Tree Frog (*Hylans cinera*)
Green Turtle (*Chelonia mydas*)
Indigo Snake (*Drymarchon corais*)
Lizard (Agamidae)
Loggerhead Turtle (*Caretta caretta*)
Marbled Salamander (*Ambystoma opacum*)
Mimic/Eastern Glass Lizard
  (*Ophisaurus ventralis*)
Mole Salamander (*Ambystoma talpoideum*)
Pine Barrens Tree Frog (*Hyla andersoni*)
Rat Snake/Black Snake (*Elaphe obsoleta*)
Spotted Salamander (*Ambystoma maculatum*)

Invertebrates

Georgia Spiny Mussel (*Elliptio spinosa*)
Marsh Crab (*Sesarma reticulatum*)
Mud Fiddler Crab (*Uca pugilator*)

Periwinkle Snail (*Littorina littorea*)
Ribbed Mussel (*Ischadium demissum*)

Arthropods

Broad-Winged Damselfly (Calopterygidae)
Deer Fly (Tabanidae)
Deer Tick (*Ixodes scapularis*)
Dog Tick (*Dermacentor variabilis*)

Honeybee (*Apis mellifera*)
Lone Star Tick (*Amblyomma americanum*)
Mosquitoe (Culicidae)
Red-Skimmer Dragonfly (Libellulidae)

PLEASE NOTE: It is understood that there is inherent risk involved in any outdoor activity, and the Environmental Protection Agency, Tennessee Valley Authority, and the author assume no responsibility for the safety of the users of this guide. While every effort has been made to check the accuracy of all information, the co-publishers and the author are not responsible for erroneous information, if any, contained in this book, nor for changes to roads, trails, or other features by agencies private or public. If you have any questions regarding the most current information for a particular wetland, please call the phone number provided within each entry.